the OTHER SIDE *of the*
JACKIE ROBINSON STORY

"BIG" ED STEVENS
Brooklyn Dodger Hall of Fame

the OTHER SIDE *of the* JACKIE ROBINSON STORY

TATE PUBLISHING *& Enterprises*

Published by Tate Publishing & Enterprises, LLC
127 E. Trade Center Terrace | Mustang, Oklahoma 73064 USA
1.888.361.9473 | www.tatepublishing.com

Tate Publishing is committed to excellence in the publishing industry. The company reflects the philosophy established by the founders, based on Psalm 68:11,
"The Lord gave the word and great was the company of those who published it."

Published in the United States of America

ISBN: 978-1-60799-112-0
1. Sports & Recreation / Baseball / History
2. Biography & Autobiography / Sports
09.08.31

DEDICATED TO OUR THREE DAUGHTERS,
Janice Kay, Barbara Sue,
and Vicki Lynn,

AND TO MY LOVING WIFE
OF SIXTY-SIX YEARS,
Margie.

ACKNOWLEDGEMENTS

Bruno Betzel, my Triple A manager, first saw me as a crude, awkward, immature kid. He chose me because he had faith that he could smooth out my fielding and hitting abilities and make me a competitive ball player, which he did. Due mostly to his managing skills and baseball knowledge, I became a Major League prospect, and I will always be grateful.

CONTENTS

LOS ANGELES Dodgers®

TOMMY LASORDA
SENIOR VICE PRESIDENT
TEL.: (323) 224-1356

1000 ELYSIAN PARK AVENUE
LOS ANGELES, CA 90012-1199

October 2, 2006

Dear Readers,

Ed Stevens and I played together in Puerto Rico during winter ball many years ago. He was a good teammate and an even better friend. He was a good player who could hit for power, but more importantly, he was the type of player that conducted himself with the highest degree of class at all times throughout his long major league career.

This book will be very interesting. Ed found himself in a position because he was a first baseman, and of course, Jackie Robinson's first position was first base. I think you will enjoy reading Ed's account of what happened, and how he was involved in this historic transformation of baseball.

Sincerely,

Tom Lasorda

Tom Lasorda
Special Advisor to the Chairman
Los Angeles Dodgers

INTRODUCTION

"How did you let a black man take your job?" This is the question I've been asked more times than I care to admit. And despite its inherent prejudice, its misunderstanding of history, its naiveté, I'm compelled to respond. This book is my answer.

My name is Ed Stevens. In baseball circles I was known as Big Ed Stevens, and I played first base for the Brooklyn Dodgers in 1945, '46, and '47. I was the first man to be replaced by a black player in the history of Major League Baseball.

My story has been dramatized, degraded, and dismissed, but never fully told. I was voted into the Brooklyn Dodger Hall of Fame, as was a man named Branch Rickey, the general manager of the Brooklyn Dodgers during my time there. He and his handshake play a large part in my story.

This is a book about the Brooklyn Dodgers, and a secret I have kept for over fifty years.

JACK ROOSEVELT ROBINSON

The first time that I ever laid eyes on Jackie Robinson—I heard they had signed a black man, but didn't pay too much attention to it—was at spring training in Havana. There was a side to Jackie that was immediately apparent. He was aware of the fact that he had to constantly prove to Leo Durocher and the Dodgers that he was capable of playing big-league ball.

The first time he came to bat he stood in the very back of the batter's box, his back foot on top of the far line, and kind of lunged at the ball. Hal Gregg, a hard-throwing right-hander, threw the first pitch, and Jackie tried to drag-bunt.

He was two or three steps out of the batter's box when he made contact with the ball and bunted it foul. Nobody thought a whole lot about it. "Okay, the man's going to try to drag-bunt." The very next pitch he tried the same thing, and to this day I don't think Hal Gregg was deliberately throwing at him.

It was a hard fastball, and Jackie ran up again but the ball was a little inside—not at him, but inside—and he ran right into it. The ball hit him in the ribs and he went down on one knee, and we could hear him sucking air.

"IF YOU MAKE YOUR BED, YOU'RE GOING TO LIE IN IT"

When I was a kid, we were poor. My mom and dad were not educated people and didn't make much money. My brothers and I grew up in a racially diverse neighborhood, and I always played football and baseball with the Mexican and African-American boys. From time to time, as kids do, we would squabble and get into fights. I was called "honky," "white trash," and the infamous M.F. word. But somehow we always seemed to work it out and still remain friends.

My older brothers rarely wanted to play with me, so when I couldn't round up boys to play ball, I created my own games. I would throw a tennis ball against the house to practice my ground balls. When I got tired of that, I would get a baseball bat and head out to the yard. We had a small tree in our yard that gave off little green berries. We called it an Achina Berry tree, though I never knew if that was its real name. The tree had one limb that was two inches thick and hung down from the side of the tree about five feet high. I would swing my bat up at the limb to try and hit the tip of the branch. I do this over and over until my arms got tired. Needless to say the tip of the limb took some abuse.

Through this practice I developed an uppercut swing, which made me a good low-ball hitter. Later in my career, when pitchers saw my upper cut, they would try to throw high pitches because they were a little harder to hit. I've had players tell me that when their club had meetings on how to pitch our team, they all used four words: Don't pitch Ed low.

The first organized ball I played was American Legion baseball from the time I was thirteen years old. By the time I was fourteen I was playing American Legion ball during the week and I would in an amateur city league with grown men on Sundays. It seemed that I hit the ball a little better with the grown men because they had better control than the American Legion boys.

Bernard Davis was my coach in those days, a Galveston-born man who never played any baseball but became a very fine student and teacher of the game. We would start out in early January and practice every day, five days a week, even though our season didn't open until April 15. That gave us a real long time to get in shape and be ready to play baseball. He knew that most of the young catchers couldn't throw too well and pitchers would take a little more time getting their delivery off, so he had a running ballclub: every time you got on first base you would steal. Nine out of ten times, we could make it, and we scored a lot of runs. When I turned sixteen I decided it was time to see if I could make it in pro ball.

I approached my dad and asked him what he thought about me playing professional baseball. "Son, you're sixteen years old. You'd going to miss an awful lot of schooling, schooling you can't get back. You think long and hard about that. If you make your bed, you're going to have to lie in it."

It didn't take me long. At sixteen, few decisions did. "Dad, I think I can play baseball."

He looked me in the eye and nodded. "Then do it. Go as far as you can and see what happens."

Soon I found myself on the West Texas & New Mexico Class D Club of Big Springs. An older fellow named Jody Tate was the manager, and he had played major-league ball as an infielder. I had written him a letter to ask for a tryout, and he agreed. I went down there as a pitcher, outfielder, and first baseman. When I got there, they did not have one first baseman in the whole camp; but they did have ten pitchers and seven or eight outfielders. So right away they told me I would have to start at first base, and after about a week they informed me that I was their first baseman to stay.

I played at Big Springs, Texas, in 1941 at sixteen years of age. I hit seventeen homeruns and drove in eighty runs. I was a sixteen-year-old boy playing with older men. During the days of the '30s and 40s, a ballplayer started out in Class D and worked his way as high as he could go in baseball. Then when he peaked out he would start going back down the ladder all the way to Class D until they wouldn't give him a uniform anymore. Here I was, a sixteen-year-old boy struggling to reach some maturity, playing with older men who accepted me.

I had a pretty good year for them, and the following year we moved to Lamesa, Texas, located about ninety miles from Big Springs. They were a franchise of Big Springs who functioned as an independent club in the Texas-New Mexico League. I got off to a good start there and was playing very well. Monty Stratton, the big White Sox right-hander who shot himself in the leg, was the manager of Lubbock, Texas, and was trying to make a comeback as a pitcher. His leg had to be amputated from the knee down. They replaced it with a peg leg that was strapped to the upper part of his leg. One of my pleasures of life was being able to meet the man and, of course, hit against him. He pitched against us that night and I hit very well against him. He could still throw the ball as hard as ever, and his breaking balls were good, but he had so much trouble handling himself that he was never able to work himself back.

I had a good year at Lamesa, but in the middle of the year was sold to the Brooklyn Dodger organization and went to Johnstown, Pennsylvania, because the West Texas-New Mexico League folded in 1942 because of the war. Johnstown was in the Penn State League. I finished up the year with them and compiled decent numbers.

About the time I got back home after the season, the war was still on, and they were starting to draft young men for the service pretty heavily. I decided to get on the involuntary retired list and wait for my draft call, which I had gotten. In the meantime, I had married a young lady from Meadville, Mississippi, Margie Lee Saxon.

During my involuntary year I had my examination for the service. As I went through the process, exams by doctor after doctor, and I got to one who asked me how I slept at night. I told him that I imagine it was as good as anybody. He asked if I had nightmares, spells, jumped up in my sleep or anything. This was something I had dealt with most of my adult life. "Yes, sir, wild horses are after me, or I'm trying to get out of the way of cars, and I sometimes ramble around the room, but that I eventually settle down."

When I got to the final, there were four officers sitting

there, Marines, Coast Guard, Army, and Navy. The first officer said, "I am rejecting this young man because of his wild sleeping habits, and his flat feet—I don't think he is eligible for service." They debated back and forth and ended up all turning me down. They decided it wouldn't be good if I jumped out of a foxhole during one of my spells.

A TALE OF TWO MANAGERS

The following year, 1944, I reinstated myself in baseball and went to spring training with the Brooklyn Dodgers. That was the first time I ever laid eyes on Leo Durocher—my first baseball nightmare.

I would give anything if I had never come into contact with that man. He was a hard-tongued, hard-nosed, insulting person who didn't like young ballplayers. He would cuss at them, tear them down in the paper, and ridicule them in front of the whole ball club. When he realized that I was a shy, immature nineteen-year-old, he rode me from the day I first put on a Dodgers uniform.

I stayed a nervous wreck all the time I was in that man's company, and I struggled through that spring training. I didn't make the Dodgers then, but I made the Montreal minor league club. Montreal had a great manager: Bruno Betzel. He was one of the best people I have ever played for. Bruno encouraged me and rounded me into a ballplayer. He told me that I was a ballplayer, and to get after it and make something of myself, and this I did. I had a respectable 1944 with them and found it easier to mature once I got away from Durocher.

The following year, however, I headed back to spring

training with the Dodgers. In 1945 we were back at Bear Mountain, New York, and I was back under Durocher again. I was playing good ball, but he had me nervous.

Hitting was my strength. I could hit for power and in the clutch. You put a man on base and in most cases I could drive that run in. I averaged close to 100 R.B.I.s every year I played in the minors.

I could always hit, but my biggest problem was my inability to handle ground balls. I was afraid of ground balls, didn't know how to approach them. But when Durocher was out of sight, I would get another teammate to hit me balls, and little by little I was starting to overcome the bad hops and learn how to handle them.

Some of the players we had on the 1945 spring training roster were Augie Galan, Eddy Stanky, Eddy Basinski, Frenchy Bordagaray, Dixie Walker, Goody Rosen, Louis Olmo, Mike Sandlock, and little Tommy Brown, one of the youngest players in the big leagues at that time. One particular ballgame stands out in my mind that spring.

Being right in Bear Mountain, New York, just on the outskirts of West Point, where they turned out all those fine officers in the academy, we would go up and play them in squad exhibition games. Of course, we would have a mixed squad going up there.

Salty Parker, who played for the Detroit Tigers, managed all over the minor leagues, and coached a lot in the major leagues, was the second baseman during our first ballgame of the spring. Our arms hadn't been stretched properly and the very first throw that I had was going start a big double play. I cranked up, put everything I had into it, but my arm locked and shoulder pain hit me, and I threw a ground ball instead of throwing it in the air to Salty.

Being the aggressive ballplayer he was, he dropped down on his knees to block the ball, and in the meantime this runner came in like a runaway freight train and hit poor ole Salty, knocking him almost out into left field. I ran over to help him up. When he got to his feet all he said was, "Ed, I want to talk to that man."

That man was the big, husky, farm-looking young man who slid into him. Salty walked over to him and said, "Aren't you a football player?"

"Yes, I am."

Salty asked if he would mind telling us who he was, and he said that he was Doc Blanchard. We hardly believed it. Doc was one of the toughest and most outstanding football players at West Point. And he'd pummeled Salty because of my inaccurate throw.

We went on and got our spring training in, and Durocher ripped me in the papers with quotes like "Stevens isn't ripe for the majors," so I knew I was heading back to Montreal once again in 1945. Frankly, I was tickled to death to get back with Bruno Betzel and away from Durocher.

In Montreal, Bruno had quite a job on his hands. Counting himself, there were four managers in the ball club. Three came back as players—Al Todd, Gus Brittain, and of course, Salty Parker—but Bruno was the manager. I used to get a kick out of them because during the ballgame Bruno would make a decision to bunt, or steal, or take the pitcher out, and they would debate amongst themselves whether or not he had done the right thing. They drove Bruno up a wall practicing their managing skills.

To show you what kind of manager Bruno Betzel was, during one game I pulled a muscle in my leg—we called them "charley horses" then. They wrapped me as tightly as they could, and I was limping around on it. Then while still playing and favoring that leg, I pulled a muscle in the other leg. Obviously I was really struggling. Then a few innings later I made a real awkward slide and sprained my wrist. I had both legs wrapped, my sprained wrist wrapped, and I told Bruno that I couldn't play tomorrow because I was hurting too bad.

Bruno Betzel said he knew I was hurting and that I wouldn't tell him I was hurting if I wasn't, but he asked a favor of me. "We are a better ball club with you in the lineup. They rally around you if you. Would you just stand at first base for me? I don't care if a hundred balls get hit to you and you make errors left and right. Would you do this for me and keep the ball club together?"

"If you'll allow for anything that may go wrong!" I said. So I played, and the very first ball was a hard hit between first and second. There I was with two injured legs and a sprained wrist, and I took after that ball and dove for it, knocked it down, and threw it to the pitcher at first base. When I came in after that inning was over, I got chewed out from one end to the other. "I thought I told you to not try for any balls, to let them go through and not hurt yourself any more!" I told Bruno that it was instinct. You play by instinct. That is why I think I became a really good ballplayer.

I was happy to play with Bruno, and I was having the best year I'd ever had. I was ready for the big leagues because Bruno encouraged me, relied on me to be part of his team, and made me a man.

"KID, YOU'RE GOING TO THE SHOW"

I was playing against big-league players in Triple A base-ball, which was a real strong league. About the middle of the season, I was hitting the best I have ever hit in my life, and in came Branch Rickey Jr. from the Brooklyn Dodgers (Branch's son), telling Bruno that they were going to take me. I was being promoted to the Brooklyn Dodgers.

All I could think about was how badly I was treated by Leo Durocher. I couldn't stand the man. He knew I could play baseball, and yet he still rode me severely.

I told Branch Jr. that I would not go to the big leagues and play for Leo Durocher. I wanted to play big-league ball more than anything, but not for him. It was the chance of a lifetime, but I couldn't force the word "yes" out of my mouth. Little Branch stayed around there for three or four days trying, and failing, to convince me to go, so he went on back to Brooklyn and told his dad that I didn't want to play for Leo.

I really was happy with my situation. I was one of the best players on the team, and I had a manager believed in me. Why would I want to go up and get abused by Durocher?

I assumed the chance had passed, but then three days later I got a visit from Clyde Sukeforth, a former major-league catcher who was a scout for the Brooklyn Dodgers. Clyde was a friendly, outgoing person I thoroughly respected and enjoyed being around. He hung around a few days trying to get me to go to the big leagues.

Bruno Betzel was getting very nervous and upset because, as he told me one night, it was his job to develop players and get them ready for the big leagues—and he knew I was ready.

I told him I would take my chances because I did not want to play with that man.

Bruno kept my wife and me up until 1:30 in the morning debating the issue. He insisted that I had to go even though he didn't want to lose me. "If you don't go, they will probably end up firing me and running you off, too."

And that's what did it. I finally realized that I was hurting him, this manager I respected so much, and for that reason alone I decided to go.

In a few days, we got on an airplane. It was the first time I had ever flown in my life and I was scared to death getting on the airplane. I was twenty years old. After two years of D ball and eighteen months of Triple A, I was on an airplane going to Brooklyn. As much as I dreaded my new manager, I was tickled to death to be going to the big leagues.

We landed in New York, started catching subways, and worked our way over to Ebbets Field. We were taken upstairs to Branch Rickey, who was in the pressroom, and given sandwiches and drinks.

"I understand that you don't want to play for me," said Branch.

"Mr. Rickey, you're wrong," I said. "I don't want to play for that man down on the field."

He said he realized that Leo was bad for young ball-players, but he told me he would back me 100% if I would go ahead and put the uniform on. If Durocher told me to change my hitting style, or not to do this or that, I was to say, "Yes, Mr. Durocher, I agree with you," and then when it came time, do it the way Ed Stevens did it.

I expressed concern about what would happen if we were in Cincinnati or St. Louis or a long way from Brooklyn. Branch assured me he would take care of it and not to worry about it. So I went down and got in uniform.

BIG LEAGUE DEBUT

When we first got to Brooklyn, Margie and I found a little place in Ozone Park, Long Island. That's where we lived our first year in 1946. We didn't have an automobile at the time, so I took the train into Brooklyn and then a subway over to Ebbets Field nearly every day. I was tickled to death to get to the ballpark, but resented the fact that I had to put the uniform on and listen to Durocher.

I never knew what scared was until I sat on the bench my first day in the big leagues. I joined the ball club about halfway through a doubleheader with Cincinnati. I got in the dugout, and it hit me that I was in a big-league ballpark, with a big-league uniform on, playing for a big-league club. They told Durocher I was there, and he gave me a very weak handshake and told me to sit on the bench and watch the rest of the ballgame. I sat there while the Dodgers were out in the field, eying everyone like I was in a candy store. Then all of a sudden Leo said, "Ed, get a bat. You're going to pinch-hit."

I said, "Okay," and just sat there.

He hollered back down and started cussing, saying, "I don't think the hell you heard me! Get a bat—you're going to pinch-hit!"

"Leo—"

"Get down in the runway behind the dugout here and loosen up and take some swings!"

I had never felt more embarrassed or awkward in my life, and on top of it I didn't know when to come in out of the runway because I didn't know if the club was still out in the field. So I took a few practice swings and finally got the courage to go back and look and see. Fortunately we got the third out just as I looked.

I was going to pinch-hit for the first hitter, Frenchie Bordagaray. I walked out for my first at bat in the big leagues, and I was spitting cotton, my adrenaline flowing and every nerve straining. To this day it was the toughest walk I've ever had.

Elmer Riddle was pitching for Cincinnati. I had worked the count to about two balls and a strike, and he threw me a big overhand curveball that started breaking down about belt high. I had an uppercut swing to start with, and I hit that ball with all that adrenaline flowing like it had been shot out of a bazooka.

That was the highest ball I had ever hit in my life—a so-called "popup" infield. The third baseman ran over, the shortstop, the second baseman, and the catcher. All of them were dancing around under the ball. I was pulling into second base when the third baseman fell flat on his back and caught the ball.

I drove twenty-nine runs and hit four homeruns in my brief 1945 season, and I went into spring training in 1946 still unsure of my position with the club. We were in Daytona Beach, Florida, and I was still fighting with Durocher. When you went into spring training, there were four, five, sometimes six people aiming for your position, trying to move up in the organization. The battle lasted all spring, but I fought everybody off and won the job as first baseman.

The 1946 season was a better one for me, at least on the field. In all the spring trainings I'd attended and instruction I'd received, no one had ever worked with me on how to approach or field a ground ball. Early in the 1946 season, Durocher told Ray Blades, one of our coaches, to hit me ground balls during batting practice and hit them hard. He did hit them hard and they were bouncing off my chest, arms, and legs. I was being eaten up by them, but I would stay with them and try to catch them all.

Pee Wee Reese, our shortstop, was one of the finest people I have ever met and played with, a gentleman all the way through his baseball career and still is today. Pee Wee walked over to me at first base, put his arm around me, his glove resting on my shoulder, and said, "Ed, the next ball he hits, put your glove down on the ground and get low with it. You can come up with your glove faster than you can go down with it."

They hit a few more balls to me, and sure enough, he was right. Before that session was over I had overcome the fear of a bad hop or a ground ball. I used that advice to conquer my trouble with ground balls and turned myself into one of the better fielders in the National League. I never let a ball get by me, and I began to love the challenge of a bad throw. I made remarkable progress in the field, and I owe a lot to Pee Wee Reese and that one little remark.

I had a nice 1946 season, driving in seventy runs and hitting ten homeruns, and I won quite a few ballgames over that short Ebbets Field fence; I was built to play in that ballpark. The team also had a nice season before losing to the St. Louis Cardinals in the playoffs.

Branch Rickey never came through on his promise to fend off Durocher. Leo was a bully, and while I felt like I often got the brunt of it, the truth was nobody liked the man.

During infield, Billy Herman would fire ground balls he had caught into the dugout to try to hit Durocher, and he would never know who had thrown it or where it had come from.

My locker was the first one as you came into our club-house. Pee Wee Reese was next to me, Pete Reiser next, and on down the line of the players. When Durocher would come in to the clubhouse, which he rarely did until fifteen minutes before the ballgame, he would come in the door, look me right in the eye, and say, "Hi, Pee Wee, hi, Pete. How're you doing?" Then he'd go on into his main office and dress.

He was not an honest man, not a decent man. On top of that, our dugout was like a three-ring circus. Durocher fancied himself a celebrity, and he constantly had movie stars, singers, actors and the like in that clubhouse. Danny Kaye, Jack Benny, Perry Como, and Groucho Marx among others were frequent visitors, and Durocher would parade them around among the ballplayers to make sure we all saw them.

You might wonder why Durocher had kept me around up until this time. The truth is Leo knew that I had some ability—I had power, could drive in runs, and hit homeruns, and when my fielding started coming around he knew that he was seeing a mature ballplayer turn into a major-leaguer. One of the few times Mr. Rickey ever complimented me, he called me the "rubber man," because he couldn't understand how a man of my height could stretch so far and go after the wildest of throws. He said I had better judgment of a bad throw than anybody he'd ever seen.

Playing for the Dodgers in that era was incredible. The Yankees at that time were winning pennant after pennant, but they were viewed as a high-class, well-paid, exclusive organization, while we were considered ordinary people. The fans loved us. They were outstanding, enthused as much as anyone could be, and they backed their ballplayers 100%. It was a pleasure playing for those people in spite of the aggravations and troubles I had in trying to get along with Leo Durocher. I wouldn't trade anything for my days as a Brooklyn Dodger.

Indeed, it was a different era altogether. The ballplayers were dedicated and loyal to their ball clubs, and most hoped to play for one club for their entire career. It was also a tough era, because every year you went to spring training, and with so many clubs around—the Dodgers had two or three Triple A clubs and two Double A clubs—if you flubbed just a little bit, there was always someone waiting to take a shot at your job. You had to be on your toes and push yourself to stay up there.

During our era there weren't as many college graduates and educated people coming into the game as now. That's not a put-down to the ballplayers, but at that time all the computers and new world sort of thing hadn't come in yet. As soon as the season was over, all of the players had to get home and go straight to a workshop to see if we could get a winter job; we didn't make enough money in the summer to sit around and fish and hunt like they do today. We were tickled to death that we were able to play ball and didn't think twice about it.

Branch Rickey was a highly educated man, and he would take some of his minor-league managers and players every now and then and get them in conversation and use such big words that nine out of ten people didn't understand what he was trying to say. He would get the biggest kick out of their answers because they had no idea what they were answering.

Branch was a very stern, strict man, and he wasn't overly liked in Brooklyn. I remember one incident in about the middle of the 1946 season when we had gotten word that the ball club was going to give all of the players brand-new Studebaker automobiles, and in return Leo and the traveling secretary, Harold Parrott, got together with us and we all chipped in and bought him a real nice pleasure boat. It wasn't one of those big oversize yachts, but you could get about six or eight people on it and cruise some pretty good waters. The only problem was they couldn't figure out how to get him to the ballpark to present the boat to him at the same time we were receiving our automobiles.

Harold Parrott came up with a plan. Carl Furillo and Leo Durocher didn't get along as well as you would like, and Hal Parrott went to Branch's office in Brooklyn and told him Leo and Carl had had a knock-down and drag-out and it had gotten so bad that he would have to go out there and straighten it out. Well, that was right down his alley, throwing his weight around and showing how he could stop everything, and so he rushed out to the ballpark.

The boat was already on the field, and Parrott told him that they were in the dugout and that he needed to go in there and talk to both of them. When he got to the dugout he realized what was going on and reluctantly went out onto the field to receive his boat, but on his way out he was hollered at and booed. That was the first time I realized that Mr. Rickey was not so well liked in Brooklyn. The fans got on him pretty heavy, but he got his boat, and we got our automobiles.

HAVANA

In 1947 we moved to Havana, Cuba, for spring training. Before we left, Rickey had sent me a contract. I was only making six hundred dollars a month at the time, and knowing how the man could debate you and argue you down, I went ahead and signed it, though it was a very weak raise. When we got down to Havana, Branch came up to me and said, "Young man, anybody that would sign a contract like I mailed to you deserves a raise. You come on back in my office, and I'll give you a raise." He'd realized his error and gave me a four-hundred-dollar raise. I was floored, as Mr. Rickey wasn't known as generous with his money.

The Yankees were down in Caracas, Venezuela, that year, so we teamed up with them a few times and played exhibition games. The first day we met up with them, I found myself on an elevator with Joe DiMaggio, Phil Rizzuto, and King Kong Keller.

I got up courage enough to say something to Joe DiMaggio. But Joe had kind of a bashful air about himself, and he looked down at the floor and said, "I don't care for talking."

We got down to the lobby, and it was a stunning sight— standing around in full uniform were Hugh Casey, Pee Wee Reese, Pete Reiser, Louis Olmo, Joe DiMaggio, Bill Dickey,

Phil Rizzuto, and Charlie Keller, just to name a few. We were assembling in the lobby before we caught our buses on out to the ballpark.

Everyone was chatting leisurely when suddenly Bill Dickey stepped off the elevator and walked up to Hugh Casey, set his glove and equipment down, and said, "Hugh, I understand you have a problem with me, and we need to settle a few things."

Hugh Casey, without flinching, looked him square in the eye. "If I had anything against, you, Bill, I would come to you—you wouldn't have to come to me," said Hugh.

Now these were both good-sized men, and we all began to back away to give them plenty of room in case sparks were going to fly.

Bill said, "Well, this is good a time as any to settle all this and get it straight. You sure there's nothing you want to talk to me about?"

"Not a thing," said Hugh.

"Fair enough," said Bill.

We all knew they would have gone to fisticuffs if it hadn't gone just right, but fortunately they settled it without a scuffle, and everyone went on about their business.

Spring training was also a chance to get into trouble, and at the Nationale Hotel there were a couple of guys having a particularly colorful vacation. Kirby Higby, one of our pitchers, wasn't exactly a "choir boy" as he loved to go out and drink, carouse, break rules, and stay out a little later than most, and he was in rare form in Havana.

One evening several of us were standing in the lobby talking with the hotel manager, and Kirby Higby was in the group. A man walked in wearing one of those Panama suits, and he spoke briefly with the manager in Spanish.

The fellow then walked on, and the hotel manager started laughing as he returned to our group. He reported that the man had asked him which one of us was Kirby Higby. When the manager asked why, and the man replied he had been hired by Branch Rickey to tail Kirby and report where he went, how late he stayed out at night, and whether he was drinking. He was a private detective.

The manager told him Kirby wasn't in the lobby right now. We got the biggest kick out of the Latin P.I. following Kirby. Branch got serious if he thought a man was breaking rules.

The other man having issues that spring was Dick Young, one of the finest and most respected writers in New York. He was covering our spring training as a sports writer. This was a big plush hotel, and well-to-do people were often spotted spending their vacations there. One particular morning, it was kind of quiet, and a tall, well-dressed, high-society-looking woman was walking down the lobby all by herself and into another area where there were sitting rooms. Dick Young recognized her, and he decided he was going to get himself a real scoop of a story by approaching this woman. She was the girlfriend of Lucky Luciano—a gangster-gambler and big-time mobster out of New York at that time—and Dick knew that Lucky was staying in the hotel.

So Dick walked up to her and tried to introduce himself, but before he got his name out, four big rough-and-tumble fellows came out of nowhere, grabbed Dick by each arm, and informed him that they wanted to know what his intentions were.

Dick turned white and didn't know what to do or say, and he finally muttered out that he was a writer and that he was just hoping to get a comment from her and maybe give her a little publicity. He was told in no uncertain terms that it was the time for him to get on and not to ever talk to the woman again. We razzed Dick all spring about his big scoop.

Our spring training facility had the minor-league clubs there, too, but they were in a separate hotel in another part of Havana and the only time we would see them was when we would play inter-squad games with them back and forth. We would place some players on the Montreal team, and Montreal would place some on ours, just to see what players looked like, get everybody in shape, and work together.

Jackie Robinson was an aggressive though not exceptional ballplayer at that time, playing second base with the Montreal club. It was apparent pretty quickly that he had a chip on his shoulder. When he was on base he would try to force pitchers to make throws over to first base, and he frequently tried to steal bases. I had no qualms about this, but some of the guys didn't care for Jackie's style. That and the fact that everyone was competing for a job in spring training made for an intense atmosphere.

There were about four to five first basemen down there at that time, and I had to battle every one of them to hold my job. When spring training ended, I had succeeded: I was the first baseman, Eddie Stanky was the second baseman, Pee Wee Reese was the shortstop, and Arkie Vaughn was the third baseman. That was the infield we were taking from spring training to open the season in Brooklyn for the 1947 season.

But while we were still in spring training, there was some

talk of Jackie Robinson. I hadn't heard much of it, but there were little rumors floating around that Jackie might eventually be put on the big club. I read in a newspaper that Durocher called the whole team out of their hotel rooms and told them that a black man was going to be on the ball club and that he had heard there was a petition going around. There has been much made of that petition, but I never saw it, never heard talk of it, and I don't know who in the world started the rumor, but then I was just a young player and nobody let me know anything.

I do know there was no way Durocher could have rounded everybody up. Leo wasn't overly fond of a black man coming on the ball club, and he had made comments to some of the coaches that he was well satisfied with Ed Stevens and Howard Schultz and the platoon system he had, so Durocher was not a bandwagon man to bring him in.

Our spring training was winding down, our ball club had been set, and everybody who was going to make the club had made the club. I had had a little better year than Howard Schultz so I was a little ways ahead of him, and as we flew from Havana back to Brooklyn, I held hopes of nailing down the regular starting job.

A BROKEN PROMISE

One day before the 1947 season began, Leo called us all into his office. "The old man says he's going to bring the black man up." He had no say about it. Rickey determined that this was what was going to happen and he wanted us all to accept it. Durocher said that he didn't particularly like it, but we would have to go along with it.

A few minutes later, we were all back at the clubhouse when Jackie Robinson walked in.

That was my second look at Jackie Robinson. He was wearing a Brooklyn Dodgers uniform. It was the first time any of us had seen a black man in a major-league uniform. It was a strange moment. No one really went overboard to greet him; in fact, a couple of young players were bawled out by the older players for even speaking to him. It was unheard of for a black man to join a big-league club. Jackie had a rough road ahead.

Little did I know it, but so did I. Though he had been a second baseman throughout his minor-league career, in the season opener, Jackie Robinson, not Ed Stevens, started at first base.

I would like to say that I realized the magnitude of the situation and happily stepped aside, accepting my role as the sacrifice in this incredibly significant moment in history. But the truth is I was competitor, and I was agitated. The fact remained that coming out of spring training the starting first base job was mine, and the rug had been ripped out from under me.

Jackie went hitless in his first game. He got a few more games, then I played a few, and so it went for that first month.

In those first few series it was obvious that Jackie was having trouble adjusting. He was trying to learn the pitches, and his timing was off. But the man never lacked in effort.

Jackie never did say a whole lot. He kept his thoughts to himself and just went about trying to do the best he could. And as time went on he worked himself into playing pretty good ball, despite the abuse he was taking. He didn't have much support, even on his own team; in those days no one wanted to be criticized for taking up with a black man.

Even after his first homerun, no one in the dugout made an attempt to congratulate him. Everyone was uneasy, and no one was sure how to handle the situation. We had no precedent.

Pretty soon word spread all over the country that Jackie Robinson had joined the Brooklyn Dodgers, and black people started jamming the ballpark to see Jackie play. Early in his career, there were as many or more black fans as white fans in the stands at Dodger games. At the time it was amazing to see that many black folks fill a ballpark. They were so proud of their man Jackie, and rightly so.

There came a stretch where I was playing and went to bat eleven times, then was benched. No big deal. But then Jackie went zero for twenty-six. No hits at twenty-six times at bat—and he kept on playing. That's when I realized there might be more to this than met the eye.

We were not competing. I began to realize that Jackie's playing time was being programmed from the front office, and every move he made was directed by Branch Rickey and his staff. People began asking me what I thought about the situation. I didn't hold anything against Jackie Robinson because he was doing exactly what he was told. But this would never have happened without Branch's tinkering. You go to spring training and fight for a job. That's how it worked. But Jackie never competed for first base. It took all I had, but I swallowed the situation. After all, I was still in the big leagues.

We were about a month into the season and it was getting close to what we called "cut-down time," when the teams cut back to a twenty-five-man roster and sent the other players back to AAA or AA. We were in Cincinnati, Ohio, starting the series with the Reds. I was in uniform, and we had already taken the field, taken our batting practice, and were in the clubhouse getting ready to come back for our infield. One of the coaches pulled me aside and told me that Mr. Rickey was sitting in a cab in the parking lot and he would like to speak to me.

I went out, in full Dodger uniform, to the parking lot. There was a cab sitting there with its meter running, and the driver was standing away from the car. Branch shook my hand and greeted me with a cordial hello. I should have seen it coming.

"Ed, I've come here all the way to Cincinnati, flew in here purposely to speak to you. What I'm going to do is ask a favor of you. Now, you've made the ball club, you're on the team, and you're an outstanding young ballplayer. But as a favor to me, I'm going to ask you to do one thing: if you would let me pull you off the roster and send you back to Montreal, I'm going to put Jackie Robinson in your spot on the roster."

I was speechless. All I could do was cross my arms as he continued.

"This will give me time enough to get rid of Eddie Stanky, who isn't good for the ball club, and Jackie belongs at second base anyway. I'll shake hands with you and give you a gentleman's agreement that this is a solemn promise. If you will do this for me, and stay in shape, have yourself a halfway decent year, or rather have a good year I should say, I will bring you back as soon as I can make a deal for Stanky."

I was sure that I was going to have to go anyway, but I told him, "Mr. Rickey, I fought all through spring training and made the ball club—I beat out five first basemen—and Jackie Robinson had not set foot in a Dodger uniform on a Dodger playing field."

I paused. He didn't respond.

"You know I can help this ball club, with the short Ebbets fence, with my power hitting, and I've improved in my fielding—"

"Ed, I know all this, but I'm telling you it will work out fine for you. I promise you will have a job for the next ten to twelve years, whatever your ability will hold up to. You've got my word, and if you will do this, I will be ever so grateful to you."

I was crushed, but I believed I had no choice. I didn't have big-league tenure, and I was afraid Rickey would just release me if I resisted.

We had already taken an apartment on Flatbush Avenue not too far from the ballpark, and my wife had all the groceries in it, and we were set up for the summer. We had just paid $110 rent for that month, and when I went in and informed the landlord that I was going to have to leave and go to Montreal, she told me there was no way she could give us our money back. The ball club didn't reimburse me.

We had managed to get an automobile at the end of 1946, so we loaded up and drove to Montreal with the understanding that I would be back as soon as he could get rid of Eddie Stanky. I was still frustrated, but I trusted Mr. Rickey's promise, and I knew I could play well and help the Montreal club. My successful return to the big club would come in no time.

"JACKIE ROBINSON'S CADDY"

There was no finer person to play ball with than Roy Campanella. He was the catcher at Montreal, and he had been up to the majors and back down like me. And like all black players in that era, he was encountering racism. After my first ballgame with the club—keep in mind that the season had been going on a month—I walked into the clubhouse and shed my uniform along with the other boys. I walked in the shower room and the players were rushing in there left and right.

There were seven or eight showers in the room, but I noticed out of the corner of my eye that there was a fellow standing in the far corner. It was Campanella. He was standing there, naked, with a washrag, toothbrush, toothpaste, and his own soap—just standing there. I realized right away what he was doing. I was a Southern boy, but I knew this wasn't right. We were teammates. I backed out of the shower and went down to him and asked him what he was doing.

He said, "Oh, Mr. Ed, I thought I would let you boys shower first. I'm in no hurry."

I grabbed him by the arm and pulled him in there and said, "Uh uh—not as long as I'm on this ball club. You're going to get in there with the rest of us. I appreciate your trying to be decent about this thing, but it's indecent, these boys keeping you out of the shower."

We got a few looks in the showers, but no one made a big deal out of it.

Roy and I became good friends as the season went along. He was an exceptional ballplayer and could have played in the big leagues right then. But the players in that day, especially the old timers, didn't like him one bit. They would slide into home and hit him as hard as they could, they would throw at him when he was at bat, and Roy would never make an effort to fight back. We would get on him and say, "Roy, you've got to take that mask and pop some of them or they're going to hurt you before it's over."

And he'd say, "No, Mr. Rickey told me to behave myself and not get in any trouble. They're not bothering me. It's okay."

Yes, Roy was a gentleman. So we decided it was up to us.

We would get some of the hardest throwers on the ball club and line them up to face all the opposing players who tried to hurt him, ran over him, threw at him. You have never seen people get knocked down worse in your life.

On out first road trip, we went into Jersey City, New Jersey, just on the outskirts of New York City, to play a Triple A club in the international league. There were 15,000 people in the stands, which was a surprise because with major-league ball clubs so close, we didn't expect a Triple A game to draw that well.

It was a night game. My first time at bat, I stepped into the box and immediately noticed a big foghorn fan sitting right behind home plate. For the first time, I felt the wrath at being sent out of Brooklyn. This man, as loud as he could holler in his foghorn voice, yelled, "There's Robinson's caddy. Hey, everyone, it's Jackie Robinson's caddy!"

It went through me like a bolt of lightning. I called time with the umpire, walked back to the stands, and I laid into the man with a verbal attack that wouldn't quit.

In the meantime, the other fans had caught wind of the joke, and 15,000 people were repeating the "caddy" remark. Realizing I couldn't fight all 15,000 of them, I went on back, and those people taunted me the whole ballgame. Then the players on the other team started riding me. "How did you let a n***** take your job?" they said.

The taunting soon spread throughout the league, and I got it at every road game. Fortunately, it didn't affect my play. Though I arrived a month late in the 1947 season, I ended up leading the league in homeruns, runs batted in, and extra base hits. Mr. Rickey said he wanted me to have a good year, and that was about as good a year as you can have.

After I finished the season at Montreal, my wife and children returned Galveston, Texas, where we were living at the time, and I went back up to Brooklyn as part of the extended forty-man roster. But Rickey brought me back three days too late to be eligible to play in the 1947 World Series.

When teams are bound for the playoffs, they rest their regulars at end of the season—let them play three for four innings, and then take them out and then let the extra men play. So they started putting me in to spell Jackie Robinson.

I wasn't above spelling somebody under normal circumstances, but I found this degrading. I won the job, was kicked down to the minors, was called back too late to be in the World Series, and then had to *spell* Jackie Robinson. But

I had no animosity toward Jackie; Branch Rickey was my object of anger.

About this time I came across an article that said the reason Rickey wanted Jackie on first was because he didn't want older players spiking him at second base. He feared that many players would intentionally harm Jackie if given the opportunity. The article also said that Jackie was surprised at this, because "that first baseman is one of your better young ballplayers on the club, and I don't think I can take his job." Mr. Rickey reportedly told him that they would work it out and not to worry about it.

I went ahead and finished out the season with them, and then while they were getting ready to play a World Series, I had to pack up and get ready to fly home. I couldn't put a uniform on and be a part it after I had, and I hate to keep repeating this, won the job. I still have pictures of the starting infield before we broke from Havana, Cuba.

I listened to the '47 Series on our radio. Galveston was a Southern town, and at that time feelings still ran high regarding black people. The people in town would get on me and some of them would avoid me because they didn't want to talk to a man that "let a n***** take his job." I apologize for using the "N" word, but that was an expression back in those days. When I grew up, I played with black and Hispanic boys—there were only a couple of white families in the neighborhood—and the word "n*****" was not abusive, it was just a name for another race. Today, as you probably know, you can get in a lot of trouble for using that word.

It was hard for a twenty-two-year-old to have to go

through all that abuse, and even today I'll see people who comment that they can't believe I let that man take my job. At the time I tried to explain that he didn't take my job; it was given to him. I practically cursed out several people around town until I finally resolved to settle down and try my best to live with it—being the white boy who let the black man take his job.

I found myself reasoning through the situation. Jackie was Branch Rickey's protégé. What would I have in Branch's shoes? He had the pressure of the world on his back, and if he had let Jackie Robinson fail, he would have probably been run out of town on a rail. And so, he put every move he had into it to see that he did not fail.

Jackie went on to have a great career, and I give him all the credit in the world. But at that particular time, Jackie Robinson could not have taken my job. I had more power, was a better fielder, and made better and more consistent contact than he did. Put simply, I was more valuable to the team.

So that winter I waited for the call, for my imminent return to the Dodgers. But they never got rid of Stanky. Then one day I picked up a paper and read that Ed Stevens had been sold to the Pittsburgh Pirates.

A PIRATE'S LIFE FOR ME

Even though I hated to leave the Dodgers, it was a good feeling to be wanted and respected in an organization. Billy Meyer, who managed Newark in the international league when I played down there, knew me real well and had a lot of respect for me, so he helped put the deal together with the Dodgers when he got the Pittsburgh job.

Hank Greenburg, the big homerun hitter from Detroit, had come over and finished the season there and then retired, so the first base spot was up in the air. When I joined the ball club, I had to compete against four first basemen. As I said before, in spring training you go fight for a spot, and whoever wins ends up on the big club.

I played hard that spring, harder than ever. I was motivated by the way I was treated in Brooklyn. And I was a worried—worried that I'd had my one shot in the big leagues and was now destined to become a lifelong minor leaguer.

Fortunately my hard work paid off. I had a great spring and won the job.

I got off to a great start with the Pirates. I started hitting right off the bat, my fielding had improved tremendously, and I was again rated one of the better fielders in the National League. I had the privilege of playing with Ralph

Kiner, Frankie Gustine, Clyde Klutz, Danny Murtaugh, Stan Rojek, Wally Westlake—players that I really admired.

At this time Ralph Kiner was hitting fifty homeruns year in and year out. When I got to the club they realized that I had some power, and they had me hitting behind Ralph. The thinking went that the other team would not pitch around Ralph Kiner if a big, strong left-hander was coming up right behind him.

Back in the 40s and 50s, when a fellow hit a homerun, the pitcher felt he had lost respect. So, many times the pitcher would try to regain this respect by throwing at the next hitter trying to knock them down. Needless to say I went down countless times a year hitting after Ralph.

Every once in awhile I would get a catcher who liked to visit when I stepped into the box, and I would tell him, "Look, let's get this first pitch out of the way, because I know I'm going to get thrown at." He would usually get a big kick out of it. And then I'd get thrown at.

I used to kid Ralph all the time. "Ralph, let me hit fourth and you hit fifth so you can get knocked down once in a while." He said he liked it just the way it was. That man could wait so long on a pitch that you would think he was going to take it, but then he would unleash his quick wrists and those long arms and the ball would take off like lightning. People would come to the ballpark early to watch us at batting practice just to see him swing the bat. Then people would stay until the ninth inning, regardless of the score, if there was any chance of Ralph getting up and hitting one last homerun. He was one of the most popular ballplayers at that time.

Another proud moment of my life was learning from

Honus Wagner, the old shortstop, one of the greatest who ever played ball. He was in his late seventies when I was with the Pirates, and he had always been involved with the franchise; as long as he was alive they kept him on salary and took care of him with all the respect in the world. Honus would put on the uniform, sit on the bench chewing his Beechnut tobacco, and visit with the players and watch the ballgame.

In one particular ballgame Howie Pollett was pitching for the Cardinals. He had exceptional control, and the first two times I was at bat he kept pitching me inside. When a ball was thrown inside and it was difficult to stretch my arms out, I would hit the ball up close to my fists or miss it altogether. Powlett just kept pouring it in on me, and I was trying and failing to get the bat around on that inside pitch. After I went back to the bench the second time, Honus asked me to come over and sit by him.

"Ed, you're having a little trouble with that left-hander, aren't you?"

"I can't keep him off of me, Honus."

"Next time you go up to bat," he said, "wait until Pollett has started his windup and can't change his delivery and is almost releasing the ball, and you take a big two or three steps away from that plate. Use your back foot and get away from the plate."

"Honus, you can't move like that in the box. You have to stand still."

He said, "Ed, if you'll do it, it'll work."

So I went back up to bat, and I was skeptical, but I took my left back foot with a big stride that got me about two and a half feet away from the plate. In came the ball, inside with a little mustard on it, and I got around on the pitch and hit it solid on the nose. I sent it into the double decks there in Pittsburgh Forbes Field, and after I rounded the bases, I came back in and sat down.

"Well, Ed, this game's not too tough, is it?" said Honus. I told him that it wasn't tough as long as I had him there to tell me how to work it out.

Honus was a real student of the game. He had done it all, and listening to his stories was a pleasure. Even though he was up in his eighties, his mind was very alert, and it was one of the highlights of my life to be around him.

Another character involved with the Pirates at that time was Bing Crosby, who was part owner. When we did our spring training in Hollywood, Bing would come out and put the uniform on and bring his boys along. He would get out and shag balls and take a little batting practice. Then we would come in the clubhouse and he would be in the showers singing. That was something you had to pay big money for at that time, and we were getting it right in our clubhouse.

With the Pirates, I was not a platooner. Durocher had insisted on a platoon system—left-handers to hit against right-handers and a right-handers to hit against a left-handers. But the Pirates turned me loose, confident that I could field and hit against anyone.

I generally played every day in Pittsburgh, but during that hot summer season Bill Meyer, our manager, would rest us every so often. On one particular day we were playing the New York Giants in the Polo Grounds. This was a scorching-hot day, and Max West spelled me at first base.

As the visitors, we sat in the third base dugout at the Polo Grounds. Three quarters of the dugout was under a little roof to shade us from the sun, but out toward left field there was an opening where the sun beamed right down on the benches.

I sat in that sunny area for the biggest part of the ball-game, and my shoes got so hot I unlaced them to let a little air in. That's how I sat there for most of the game, my shoes unlaced and my glove in my pocket.

Well, as tends to happen with anyone sitting with the sun shining on them, I started getting a groggy, and the next thing I knew my head had dropped to my chest and I was taking a little nap. In the meantime, Danny Murtaugh, our second baseman, was due at bat again with a couple of men on base, and Bill said, "Ed, get a bat."

Well, in my little napping session, I didn't hear anything. One of the players sitting next to me nudged me with his elbow and said I had better wake up because the skipper wanted me. I asked what he meant. Finally Bill hollered down to get a bat because I was going to pinch hit. Well, that startled out of my stupor and I shook myself a little and stood up. "You had better tie your shoes," said someone.

I laced up, pulled my glove out of my pocket, and grabbed a bat. Meanwhile, Danny Murtaugh, who I was pinch hitting for, and who was having an outstanding day, was pretty upset, and he took his bats and slammed them against the bat rack.

Clint Hartung, the young man pitching that day, was a big gangly-armed right-hander who threw hard. I walked on up, still trying to get myself together, and took a couple of practice swings. Then I stepped in.

Hartung threw as hard as anybody at that time, but he laid that thing right down in my power zone. With most of your hard throwers, the ball would rise or sail to the side a little, but Clint's fastball just stayed as straight as he threw it. I normally didn't swing at a first pitch, but I unwound on that thing and got it solid.

At the Polo Grounds there was a big Chesterfield sign in centerfield on the upper deck rail. This ball cleared that rail by twelve rows and bounced around in there. The homerun drove in three runs to put us ahead, and we went ahead and won the ballgame.

When I got back to the dugout, the players started kidding me. "Ed, go on back down there and finish your nap. You've done your job for the day!"

Murtaugh said, "I'll never question Billy Meyers pinch hitting Ed for me again." It was one of the rare times in my life that I have ever dozed off during a ballgame, but I suppose it paid off.

I had gotten off to a good start, hitting .365 and leading the American and National Leagues in runs batted in. But there was one date I had circled on my calendar that year. The Dodgers were coming, and I had something to prove.

RETURN OF THE DODGERS

Leo Durocher had been suspended for most of the 1947 season. Branch knew that Leo did not like blacks, and he was afraid to let him manage Jackie. Durocher was seeing gamblers, and word was that upon Branch's request the commissioner, Happy Chandler, agreed to suspend him based on that suspicion. Most of us on the team knew he was not suspended because of gamblers; he was suspended because he didn't like black people, and Branch knew it.

Jackie went on to have a great '47 season and won over just about everyone, so it would have been obvious prejudice if Durocher had benched him upon his return. Jackie was still playing first base when the Dodgers came to Pittsburgh to play a series in 1948. But I was more concerned with my former manager.

During my first at bat, Herb Palica, a hard-throwing right-hander, was on the mound, and just as I stepped into the box, Durocher ran up to the top step of the dugout and said, "Herb, stick one in his ear!"

I called time with the umpire. He wanted to know what I was calling time for. "I have to take care of something," I said. I walked over to the Dodger dugout, Leo glaring at me the whole time.

I stopped ten feet from the dugout and cleared my throat. "Let me tell you something, you sorry, low-life scum. I'm not your whipping boy anymore, and I don't have to put up with any of your crap, and if Herb Palica comes anywhere near me with this next pitch, I'm coming straight over here."

He started to come out of the dugout. Then he hesitated, thinking about his recent suspension no doubt, and changed his mind.

I said, "Leo, that's the smartest thing you ever did in your life."

Now Palica and I had been friends when I was with the Dodgers; in fact, we sort of chummed around together as teammates. He didn't come close to throwing at me, and I stepped in and hit a double. My vengeance was complete.

Several of the Dodgers asked me the next day why I hadn't gone in and gotten Durocher. They said they wouldn't have laid a hand on me, would have just let me have him. They wanted to somebody get that man. But I was satisfied with what I had said, and I finally felt I had Leo Durocher off my back for good.

As I said, Jackie Robinson was still playing first base since taking my place in 1947. Jackie had come into the white man's world as a baseball player, and I believe he harbored some hard feelings toward white people for what he had gone through, and I can't blame him—the man took a beating.

Jackie was always doing little things to intimidate and aggravate the opposing team. He wasn't exceptionally fast, but he was quick on his takeoff, and when he was on base he would deliberately draw throws over to get in a rundown.

Jackie would take a running start toward second base, and the first baseman would start chasing him toward second. Then as soon as the ball was thrown Jackie would turn around on a dime and come back as hard as he could with elbows and knees and run over the first baseman. Nearly every time the umpire would call interference and automatically give him second base.

Jackie would do that every time he got on base. I don't know any way to explain it except to say that it was his way of getting back at everyone. He would never challenge a pitcher for hitting him with a ball; he would never challenge someone who supposedly roughed him up other than to sometimes get in the dugout and holler. His preferred method was to run you over. I had watched this happen several times, and always hoped it wouldn't happen to me.

In a series with the Dodgers later that year, I was playing first base, and I knew what was coming. Sure enough, he took off, I got the throw, and I gave the ball to second base in plenty of time. Jackie turned around and came back at me. I didn't have the ball, and it felt like it floated in the air forever, but I got it back just before he reached first.

And on he came, those elbows and knees riding just as high as he could pump them. Thinking quickly, I sidestepped him, made a fist out of the ball, and tagged him in the stomach. I wasn't deliberately trying to hurt him, but it did knock all the wind out of him.

I said, "Jackie, I knew what you were going to try to do to me, and I had to tag you that hard to keep you from hurting me." True to form, he didn't say a word. Jackie Robinson just played himself.

He was abused a great deal, especially by the older ballplayers. The benches all rode him, and I knew what that was like. I give Jackie a lot of credit, and I hold no hard feelings against him in any shape or form. In fact, outside of that run-down, Jackie and I got along. We spoke to each other before and after games. My wife, Margie, and his wife, Rachel, sat together at the games and visited, and there were no hard feelings one way or the other.

A lot of people felt like I should hate the man, but I don't hate him because he had little say in what happened. He paid me all kinds of compliments, saying that he couldn't take my job on account of my being an exceptional young first baseman.

Jackie went on to make the Hall of Fame, and I am proud for him for what he did both as a man and as a baseball player. Whenever I've been asked over the years if I hated him, I always reply, "No, I don't hate him. Jackie showed himself to be a fine player and a good man."

FORTY-TWO DAYS

Toward the end of the 1948 season I started coming up with terrific pains in all of my joints—my shoulder joints, which affected my throwing, and my hips, which affected running, swinging, and most other movement. This cut down on my ability to play, and my batting average plummeted from .365 to .240. My body was stiffening up to where I didn't have the quick reflexes and the good coordination I used to.

I played through this for a while, not knowing what in the world was working on me. Then about three quarters of the way through the season I went in to Billy Meyers's office. I told him I was hurting so bad I couldn't swing the bat, couldn't reach my arm up for throws. He said he hated to take me out of the lineup, but suggested that I go to the hospital to see if they could find out what was wrong.

I was in the Pittsburgh hospital for fifteen days. They ran every test they could possibly run on me and could not come up with a thing. I put the uniform back on and would pinch hit and play occasionally, in pain.

By the end of the year I had driven in seventy runs, hit ten homeruns, and led the league in fielding average that year with .996. I was in 128 ballgames for the Pittsburgh Pirates, and I made only four errors out of 1,108 plays—both ground balls and thrown balls. But the stats were little consolation.

I went home that winter and did everything I could. They sent me to the Mayo Clinic in Baltimore and the Osner Clinic in New Orleans during the off season, but no one could find the source of the pain.

I came back for spring training in 1949, and I still had the same pain and situation pulling on me. I tried everything in the world to be myself, but I just couldn't swing the bat properly, it hurt to throw the ball, and it hurt to reach for a ball.

I started the season playing in pain, but after a couple of painful months I went back to Billy again. "Bill, I have to talk to you again. I haven't whupped this thing yet."

I went back in the hospital again for sixteen days this time, and again they did every possible test trying to break up adhesions or whatever they thought it might be. I was really getting despondent and could hardly live with it, but there wasn't a whole lot I could do about it, and nobody could tell me what was wrong. I knew my career was in jeopardy, but I fought it and made it through that 1949 season in one piece.

I came back in 1950 in the same predicament. I made the ball club and played the first few games with them, but by then they realized they were going to have to send me back to the minor leagues to see if I could work it out there. So, off I went to Indianapolis in the middle of 1950.

I continued to play through the pain and actually had a decent year, and in 1951 I came back with Indianapolis again and had one of the strangest experiences of my life: I got on a hitting streak that just went on and on and on.

Sometimes I would only get one hit—one for five, one

for six, one for four—but the streak kept going. I used one particular bat through during this time, and I broke it eight times. Each time this happened, my teammates would run in the clubhouse, put some nails in it, put it back together, and have it ready for my next at bat.

During one sunny Sunday afternoon game, I came to bat for the first time and when I stepped into the box the plate umpire called time.

"Ed, let me talk to you just a minute," he said.

"What kind of problem do we have here?" I asked.

He told me that he knew I had a hitting streak going, but that I knew the rule was I wasn't supposed to have any nails in any bat; nothing could be put on a bat but rosin. "I won't complain about the nails," he said, "but this sun is hitting them, and the glare is hitting my eyes so I can hardly see to call the ballgame." We got a big kick out of that. I had sixteen nails in that bat when I finally broke my streak after thirty-six games.

During the thirty-seventh game, I hung out three hard line drives and backed the centerfielder back up against the right centerfield wall so he had to jump for the ball. Ironically, I'd hit the ball extremely well on the day my streak ended.

I was still playing in pain, but thought I could work through it. In 1951 I met a doctor in Shreveport, Louisiana. He was an eye, ear, and nose specialist and plastic surgeon. In the meeting with him, he examined me and looked at my nose, which had been broken two or three times. He found that it was crushed almost shut on one side, causing breathing difficulties. He told me that I didn't have any business wearing a nose like that and that he could operate on it and straighten it, which would increase my breathing power. He said, "With a straight nose you could get a job as an actor." I told him I didn't want to be an actor, but if he could straighten my nose and ease my breathing, I would do it.

He had to do the operation in three parts because the nose was so out of whack. He took pieces of bone out of a bottle, put them in there, sawed some off, cut some out, put some in, replaced this, and straightened the nose up. When he had the nose torn down and could see into my head, he spotted the problem that had been causing all the pain in my joints. What he discovered back behind the palate in my mouth up to eye level (I didn't even know the throat went that high) was a mass of poisonous corruption.

He said, "Ed, I think I have found your problem. You've got a big infection in there." After he put my nose back together, he waited until it was healed sufficiently and went back in there with a curved knife and a light, and he cut out an area that you could have dropped a silver dollar in. It was an infection that had been dripping poisonous pus into my system, which had settled in my joints and caused all the pain. And so after four years and forty-nine doctors, this man finally found the source of the problem.

He showed me what he had taken out and said that if all that poison would have hit me at one time it would have killed me. Fortunately, it was such a gradual thing that my body was absorbing it and doing away with it before it caused any real harm, other than the joint pain of course.

He said that in one year's time I would be myself again, to let the poison work itself out of my system, and I would be the all player I once was. I was tickled to death. I finally found out what my illness was, but it had gotten me out of the major leagues and I had to go back to the minor leagues to prove myself and get that poison worked out of my system. And just as he had said, in one year's time, I did bounce back.

I tried everything in the books to get back to the major leagues, because I knew I could play major-league ball. In the meantime, the Indianapolis club had sold me over to Toronto, an independent club that was owned by Jack Kent Cook, who was a Canadian millionaire even in 1962, the year I went over there. He eventually moved to the States and owned Washington Redskins football team for quite a few years.

I played five years with Toronto in the international league. I had outstanding years, drove in over one hundred runs every year, hit thirty-five homeruns, and exhibited exceptional fielding. When the major-league scouts would come through scouting us—they all scouted the minor leagues to see what they could trade for—everyone of them told me that I could play major-league ball, but that I had a reputation of having a back problem and they couldn't take a chance of it reoccurring if they made a deal and bought me back to the big leagues.

I was really down on major-league scouts. I couldn't understand why they would think that because after my surgery I had played every ballgame, even the exhibition games, and hadn't missed a training day, and my numbers were the best in the league. I just kept playing my minor-league career because no scout would take a chance on me.

Of course, looking back I realize what those scouts were doing; I scouted for twenty-nine years after my playing days were over, and if I had been in that situation, I would have had to do the same. Unfortunately, at that time it cost me a lot more than a shot at the big leagues. In an ironic twist of fate, I was forty-two days shy being eligible for a major-league pension. Forty-two was Jackie Robinson's number.

"COACH" STEVENS

I have a big oversized 1946 Brooklyn Dodgers picture in my trophy room. Every year I go check out that picture, and each year I cross out another teammate that has left this world. At this writing, including coaches, trainers, road secretaries and of course all the players, twenty-one have passed on.

After fifty years, you would think that we old ballplayers from that era would just fade and more or less be forgotten, but each year since my playing days my fan mail has actually increased. I'm getting more fan mail than I did in the earlier years, and the nicest letters from these people, complimenting me on my baseball ability, complimenting me on playing in the era when ballplayers were ballplayers. I get lots of "my dad told me about you" letters. And the most complimentary thing is getting letters asking me to sign pictures. I've even had people send me checks telling me to sign any amount I want for signing balls or pictures. Of course I stick those back in an envelope, sign their pictures for them, and write them back: "I do not sign anything for money. If you're a good enough fan and think enough of me to request this, I'm glad to do it."

I've gotten those little bubble gum cards and eight by tens. I've even had bats shipped to me, and a dozen baseballs requesting signatures, and I'm tickled to death to do it. We're still being remembered, I appreciate every one of those people that takes the time to write and remember.

————————————

I scouted for the San Diego Padres for six years. Jack McKeon was the general manager of the Padres, and he promised that as soon as he found the right opportunity he would see that I got my time. So Jack got hold of me one day and told me to get all my scouting in order, see as many players as I could, and then report to San Diego the last week of spring training. He said I would put the uniform on and be the Padres' fifth coach.

In the meantime they had held a meeting of the four coaches—all you were allowed was four. In order for me to be the fifth, one had to take himself off the pension plan. Eddie Brinkman, one of the finest people I have ever met, volunteered. I will always respect that man as a gentleman and a friend. He pulled himself off and let me get on the major-league pension plan to get the forty-two days I needed. He had a broken year, but when he put himself back on after I left he could continue his plan.

I joined the club and hopefully did a fair job coaching and helping out any way I could. They gave me forty-four days just to overlap the forty-two. And after thirty years, I finally had the major league pension plan.

————————————

It was a sad day when they moved the Dodgers from Brooklyn to Los Angeles. I know there were a lot of upset people because that was one of the most exciting baseball clubs at that time—mostly because the fans were a very excitable bunch of people. It marked the end of an era, and I understand Ebbets Field has been torn down and now an apartment building sits on the field where we used to play. At times I wish we could all go back to that era and be frozen in time, but then nothing stays the same. I have such wonderful memories of the colorful Brooklyn fans, playing in Ebbets Field, getting acquainted with people, and being known as a Brooklyn Dodger.

I hope my story will shed some light on the history of baseball. There has been much made of Jackie Robinson's legend, and he deserves all of the glory, awards, and accolades he's received. I'm proud of Jackie. But I still wish we could have truly competed for that spot.

ADDENDUM: TALES FROM A LIFE IN BASEBALL

The Playoffs

In the 1946 playoffs, we played the St. Louis Cardinals. It was a dramatic series, and one of the most watched playoffs that I can recall.

The first game they played Howard Schultz and we got beat in St. Louis and flew back to Brooklyn. I played in the second game and faced little Murray Dickson, a fine little right-handed pitcher who threw all sorts of pitches. My first time up, I had a couple of men on, and I got hold of one of his curve balls and drove the thing as hard and high as you could possibly hit a ball.

Now, anyone that's familiar with Ebbets Field knows there's a double-decker stand going all the way from the left field foul line to the tip of center field. This ball I hit was deep center field, and it was in high enough and hard enough that it landed in the double decks upstairs, hitting a guardrail and going on into the ballpark. It was hit hard enough for a homerun, but the ruling was that it was still in the ballpark, so I ended up with a triple and drove in two runs during that ballgame.

We ended up losing the two-out-of-three series to the Cardinals, but it was one of the proud moments of my career to have played in that playoff game. We could have very easily won it, but I had to pack up and come on home to Galveston for the rest of the winter.

Branch's Wager

One afternoon several of us players had a talk with Branch Richey, Jr., Branch's son, in the back of the clubhouse.

"You know, Branch, your daddy may have set off a keg of worms bringing the first black ballplayer in." His said that his dad had run a big survey of black ballplayers, and he didn't feel like there were over four or five of them that could ever play major-league baseball, and not to worry about that baseball would never be flooded with black ballplayers.

I believe Branch Rickey would turn over in his grave today because down deep he didn't think black ballplayers had any ability or even belonged in sports. As far as I can tell, it's worked out pretty well for them. I've done a lot of major-league scouting and you see a little dissension here and there, but overall it's being handled well enough, certainly nothing compared to the treatment black ballplayers coming up through the minors received in Jackie's era.

The End of My Career

I did not leave the major leagues due to lack of ability. My health conditions forced me out, and as I mentioned earlier in this story. In the 1946 season, I had 310 at bats and drove sixty RBIs playing part time. By comparison, Pete Reiser had 423 at bats, a little over one hundred more than me, and drove in seventy-three runs. I was a good clutch hitter, and a good fielder. My career was put in jeopardy because of Mr. Rickey's plan for Jackie Robinson.

In 1947, Branch Rickey sent me to Montreal with the promise that I would be brought back so long as I had a fair year and stayed in shape. I joined the Montreal club after they had already played one month. In 133 games, I had 133 hits, 244 total bases, twenty-two doubles, four triples, twenty-seven homeruns, 108 RBIs, and I stole five bases. (I wasn't exactly a gazelle, but I could run well enough at times to steal a base.) It was the best full year I had put together. But apparently it wasn't enough.

D. J. Ed

I mentioned Jack Kent Cook, the owner of the Toronto club, several times. He also owned two radio stations, published about a dozen magazines, and was a millionaire over and over by the time he was forty-two years old. One day I was sitting around talking to some of his radio people and mentioned how much I loved western music, and that some day I would like to be a disk jockey on western radio. Well they told the boss about that, and he told them to bring me in. They started schooling me, and they were trying to capitalize on two things: I a big-name ballplayer for the Toronto ballclub at that time, and I had a Southern accent. Being all the way up in Canada, people always tried to get me to talk more to hear my accent.

He finally schooled me enough to where I got myself a radio program one day a week. I played western music, did my own commercials, and on Sundays they hosted "The Ed Stevens Show," and I would play the best western numbers, hymns, and religious numbers by people like Ernest Tubb and Eddie Arnold.

During the five years I did that program, my ratings for a disc jockey for western music showed I was drawing 51% of the listening audience in a five-station area of listeners. I was proud that went over so well for me, and since I was just playing music that I liked to hear, it was a pleasure for me to do it. I hated to leave Toronto when I was sold over to Charleston, West Virginia, after five enjoyable years.

Legends of the Game: Ben Chapman, Honus Wagner, and Ty Cobb

During the years that I played, one gentleman stands out in my mind above all the others. Benjamin Chapman was born in 1908 in Nashville, Tennessee, and was an outstanding ballplayer for the New York Yankees. He played fifteen years in the majors with New York, Boston, Cleveland, and Brooklyn. I first met him in 1944.

Ben had been one outstanding player and was a little on the tough side. He was friendly when needed to be, but was not shy about making a fist. When Ben was playing with the Yankees, the Washington Senators had several Cuban ballplayers on their roster, some of them playing every day. Well one particular game Ben was on second base, and as he started taking his lead off the bag, the little second baseman walked up to him and said, "Hey, Chappie, lookie what I got." He had the ball hidden in his hand.

When Ben looked around and realized what had happened to him, he punched that poor little Cuban, knocked him halfway across the field. He didn't care for the hidden ball trick.

Being a dyed-in-the-wool Southerner, Ben wasn't overly fond of black ballplayers, and when he was managing the Phillies and I was still with the Dodgers, he would make some raunchy and raw statements to Jackie. In fact, he got out of hand with it at one point that the baseball commissioner called him in and threatened to fire him if he didn't ease up. I think Ben finally calmed down, and I'm not trying to put him down by making this statement; back then, to Southerners, a black player was still a black man, and they were taught to snub the entire race. Fortunately since that time the gate has been opened and there is opportunity for a player to prove himself without having to worry about prejudice.

I got a kick out of Ben, not the fact that he got on black people, but that he spoke exactly what he was thinking, even if it set him back a little bit.

Ben was also a good storyteller. He once told me about the time he was playing centerfield, and Babe Ruth, in his prime, was playing right field. This particular ballgame, Ben said that they had a little small second baseman, and of

course Babe was a big, stout, strong, 200-pound man playing right field, and a little pop fly was hit out behind second
base, halfway between the second baseman and Babe at right
field. They both came running in on the ball, and the little
fellow had his back to Babe, trying to catch the ball; Babe
was looking at the ball and not paying any attention to the
fact that he was gaining on the little guy or who was going
to catch the ball.

Babe and this little second baseman ran together, and
they were no match for each other. The second baseman was
knocked out, and they had to work with him up a storm, and
Ben said that when he looked around after the little fellow
had fallen and knew he was hurt, Babe dropped down on one
knee and fell flat on his back.

Ben went running over and said, "Now, Babe, there's no
way in the world you can be hurt. What in the world are you
doing on the ground?"

Babe said, "Ben, I'm going to teach you all about sportsmanship." And Ben asked him what he was talking about,
"sportsmanship." "Just watch," said Babe. Then he came up
on one knee and the crowd started clapping, he came up on
both knees, and finally pulled himself slowly up, and when
he stood up he got a standing ovation from the crowd. While
he was waving to the croud he looked over at Ben and said,
"That is sportsmanship, my young man."

When Ben was a coach at the National League in
Toronto, Burley Grimes was the manager. You old-timers
will remember Burley Grimes was one of the best spitball
pitchers that ever came along. He won many a ballgame,
but it wasn't long after that that the pitch got so danger-
ous they finally outlawed it. I've only faced two or three in

my career, and I don't care to face any more. Burley would chew tobacco, make the ball real slick with tobacco juice or saliva, and when he threw it the ball did o not turn—the wind would catch those strings, and the ball either broke into you or away from you, down or up. Of the ones I saw there was no way I could swing at them because I had no idea which way they were going to go. Burley Grimes—the spitball king—is in the Hall of Fame now. He was one of the best.

Another old-timer, a great ballplayer who proved a real welcome and cherished friendship was Honus Wagner. Honus, as I said earlier, would come to the ballpark just like a regular ballplayer, come the same time as the ballplayers, put on the full uniform—the outer socks, the sweat socks, uniform, baseball shoes, cap and everything—and sit on our bench. Honus would move up and down the bench, and if one of us was in a slump he would ease up alongside us and talk about things.

Honus was bow-legged, he didn't really have an athletic body, but he was strong as a bull with big shoulders and strong arms, and with that little old bow-legged walk he didn't look much like a ball player, but he could definitely play ball. He would sit there chewing his Beechnut tobacco and spit all over the dugout. Everybody loved him and wouldn't take anything for the friendship with him.

Honus told me once that during his era there was only one umpire, and he stood behind the pitcher's mound and called the balls and strikes, and if a ball was hit to the outfield he would have to run halfway out to see if it was a fair catch or what they were doing with it. He said that one team had an old rough-and-tumble fellow who would do anything to beat you and didn't care how he did it. When an umpire ran out on a fly ball to see if it was caught fair and had his back to the infield, this runner would take off from first base and cut right across the mound and slide into third base, and the umpire couldn't call him out because he didn't see what happened.

Honus got tired of that, and he told his third baseman, "Look, when he comes across that mound again, you run up there and trip him and hold him down and sit on him, so the umpire can see what he's doing."

This fellow was a kind of small player, and he told Honus that that was a pretty good-sized man and that he had a little family and was trying to make a living playing baseball and that he didn't believe he had better take a chance on that. He told Honus to play short stop, and he would play third. Soon enough this fellow started from first across to third without bothering second base, and Honus said that he ran up to him and took his foot and kicked one of his legs out from under him and just sat on top of him on the mound. And it worked. The umpire called him out for not running the bases properly.

Honus was a real student of the game, you might say, because he had done it all, and listening to his stories was a pleasure. One story he liked to tell was about Ty Cobb. During their peak years, they never liked each other, and I have never heard a story yet where anyone cared anything about Ty Cobb. He was a brutal, mean man who tried to hurt people, and I've heard that he would file his metal cleats down to a sharpness just like a blade. It's said that he loved to spike people, step on their feet, stick a shoe in your chest if he was sliding into you.

Honus told me about a time when Ty Cobb got on first base while Honus was playing second. Cobb hollered out: "Dutchman, you had better get the hell out of the way because I'm coming down, and I'm going to take you out." Honus said that he just listened to him and didn't say anything, and on the very next pitch, Ty Cobb took off. But Honus said they had a catcher that had one of the strongest arms in the league, and he fired the ball down there, and Honus got it and had the man by at least ten feet waiting on him. When Cobb slid in, trying to take out Honus Wagner, Honus sidestepped him, made a fist with the ball, and busted his mouth open, loosening some of his teeth in the process. Honus said, "What took you so long to get down here?"

Legends of the Game: Don Drysdale, Tommy Lasorta, Rip Sewell and Ted Williams

When I was playing with Toronto, Montreal was still the Brooklyn Dodgers' Triple A club. Several of the players they had at that time turned out to be outstanding with the Dodgers. One was Don Drysdale.

Now, Don Drysdale was a tall, skinny, lanky boy who didn't even look healthy he was so thin. He had a loose, free arm and could throw hard, and he was just learning to pitch down there and of course didn't have real good control, but he developed into one of the better pitchers in the National League with the Brooklyn Dodgers.

Another one that became pretty big in his time was Johnny Podres, a left-hander who also could throw hard and had a good breaking ball. When I faced them they were just learning the business and they hadn't matured completely. They were learning how to hit spots, make their pitches work, change, and work over big-league hitters.

Another pitcher with the Montreal club was Tommy LaSorta. Tommy was a left-hander who didn't throw all that hard, but he had an outstanding overhand breaking curve ball. He could start the thing about letter high, and by the time you started to swing at it, it was down around your knees. You almost had to get on the plate to catch it before it started that big break. Tommy wasn't gifted with that major-league athletic body, but the ability he had he got the best out of it and was highly competitive—in fact, there were occasions when he felt the need to knock somebody down.

I was knocked down a few times, along with some of the better hitters on the Toronto Club. We had a big right-hander named Ray Shore who was hard throwing. He never had much break, but he could almost overpower you with a blazing fastball. Like I said, Tommy had knocked down a few of our hitters earlier in the year, and in one particular ballgame, Tommy was pitching, and the first time he came to bat Ray Shore, as hard as he could throw, lowered the boom on Tommy LaSorta, and he just barely got out of the way of one of the hardest fastballs I had seen thrown that year.

He got up off the ground and shook himself, just thankful he hadn't been hit, and he backed out and hollered out to Ray Shore, "Ray, I'm gonna be honest with you, I forgot all about knocking some of your hitters down, and you gave me what I deserved, and it was a good one." So there weren't any hard feelings—that was just the way of evening the score back then. If someone got knocked down, you ended up knocking them down. I've seen the time they had to take a pitcher out and wouldn't let him hit because they were afraid a good hard thrower would get him good. It was the normal thing back then. I never saw any fist fights or back throwing. We just accepted it, and if you got hit you just went on to first base knowing it was all part of the game.

Tommy LaSorta was competitive all right, but he never quite the stuff and reached the Dodgers in what we called "a cup of coffee." He was up maybe one or two or maybe three ballgames at the height of his career, but as you know Tommy blossomed out as a Brooklyn Dodger manager and was what they called the ambassador of baseball. He always said that he was such a dyed-in-the-wool Dodger that when he cut himself, his blood was Dodger blue.

Another character I played with in Pittsburgh was Rip Sewell. Rip is the man who developed what he called a "blooper" ball. Rip could throw that thing about fifteen feet up in the air, a looping, fly-ball type of thing, and he had a knack for getting it to drop in for a strike. It was a sight to see.

Little Dom Dalasandro, a short outfielder with the Chicago Cubs, was the first one that Rip ever pulled this on. Rip told the umpire what he was going to do and to be on the lookout for it, so he ran a count on Dalasandro and got two strikes on him, and here came the blooper ball. He threw the thing fifteen feet up and Dalasandro froze because he didn't know what in the world Rip was doing. Eventually the ball dropped in the strike zone and the umpire called him out on the third strike. Dalasandro was so confused and upset he took his bat and pointed it at Rip like it was a rifle. "Rip, I ought to shoot you for doing that." That's when Rip realized he had a novelty pitch and he began using it on special occasions.

A few years later in an All-Star Game Ted Williams was in the lineup for the American League, and it was Rip's turn to pitch. Rip ran a count on Ted and decided it would be a good time to try the blooper, if nothing else for a little humor. So he threw that big looping thing up in the air and it came down. Ted Williams, on of the best hitters in the game, saw what the ball was doing, waited on it, and upper-cut it right out of the ballpark for a home run. The crowd went crazy, and Rip was still glad he got the chance to show off his blooper ball.

Legends of the Game: Ty Cobb and Danny Murtaugh

Another one of my teammates on the Pirates was utility man Danny Murtaugh. Danny was an exceptional fielder, but his hitting had always held him back from becoming a regular on a major-league ballclub. One This particular spring, 1948, we had a young second baseman named Monty Basgall. He had come over from the Dodgers in a trade that winter. He was an exceptional fielder and had one of the quickest releases on a double play—that ball would be in his glove and out before you could even realize he had even caught it.

Basgall had won the job and was a regular second base-man, and Danny Murtaugh was the utility man again. Unfor-tunately, old Monty came down with either flu or pneumo-nia and was sick enough that he couldn't play and had to stay home a few days. So they put Danny Murtaugh in. Up until that time, Danny hadn't hit all that much in his career, but he started making plays at second base, turning double plays. He decided to choke up on the bat to be a contact hitter, and he started making contact and moving the ball around a little bit and getting on base. After Danny's performance, poor ole Monty never did get back in the lineup. Danny took the job for the rest of the year and he had it.

As the season went on, and as I tell this, I feel that Danny played a part in my failure to make this play I'm going to speak of. We were playing the Boston Braves; they had a man on first and second and a right-handed hitter was up hitting. I was playing a normal first base, back in the normal position, and a right-handed hitter came up and hit the ball on what we called "on the fist," just about on the trademark of the bat. It was a lazy, looping fly ball that didn't get more than twelve feet in the air.

It was going to land right on the edge of the grass and the dirt infield, and I made a charge at it. The runners held up to see if the ball was going to be caught. But the ball started falling at a faster pace than I had planned on, and I had to run and lunge at the ball. I finally caught it about six inches off the ground, so the batter was out.

Well, the last thing those two runners saw was the ball close to the ground, so they took off because they thought it dropped. The man on second slid into third, the man on first slid into second. When I caught the ball it startled me that I could even get to it and my first reaction was to double the man off at first, so I ran to the bag and tagged the base, which put out the first base runner who had slid into second. In the meantime, the runner was still on third before he realized what was going on.

Danny Murtaugh ran up and got right in my ear and as

loud as he could yelled, "Run it, run it!" It startled me, and I realized what he was trying to tell me, and I started running toward second base. The runner at third was trying to beat me back to second. I had gotten about three quarters of the way there and I would have beat him, but fear came over me and I thought that I had better go ahead and make my throw, so I threw the ball to the shortstop to make it a triple play. Danny and them got all over me, asking why I hadn't kept running with the ball. I told them that I had wanted to make sure, even though I would have loved to have had that unassisted triple play. And his hollering in my ear didn't help.

Legends of the Game: Ed Head, Vic Lombardi, and Dixie Walker

We had one pitcher on the team named Ed Head. Ed was from Monroe, Louisiana. He was originally a left-handed thrower, but he was in an automobile accident and crushed his left arm where he couldn't throw. So, he taught himself how to throw right-handed so well that he became a major-league pitcher. I played in one ballgame when Ed pitched a no-hitter, and he was sharp as a tack.

Rex Barney, a hard-throwing right-hander, could throw about like Nolan Ryan did during recent years. Rex only had two problems: his ball was straight as a string, and he had the poorest control of any pitcher I had ever been around. I played in games when he walked as many as fourteen batters. He never tried to improve himself, and I always wondered why a man with that kind of ability didn't try to help himself any more than he did. He did go on to win a few games for the Dodgers later on, so I assume his control eventually came around.

Another one was little Vic Lombardi. He was just about a Bobby Shantz in size.

Little Vic had a habit of pulling the bill of his cap down so far you wondered that he could even see out from under it to throw. Vic was real small in size, but when he released the ball, he had a last minute wrist snap that threw the hitters off because they saw the motion, and they were hitting at the motion. But when he flipped that wrist, he picked up speed and was an effective left-handed pitcher to be as small as he was.

Pete Reiser was one of the better ballplayers on the club. "Mr. Hustle," about like a Pete Rose. He could play the outfield, he could hit, he could get on base, he could bunt, he could steal bases. Pete's only problem the brick wall at Ebbets Field. Anytime there was a fly ball near that wall, instead of backing up to the wall to catch the ball, he would stand about three or four feet from the wall and jerk himself backwards to catch the ball, and by the force of his falling backwards to catch the ball, he would hit his head on that cement. He cracked his head several times and had to be taken to the hospital.

Eddie Stanky, broke the walks record. He got more walks getting on base with a walk. He would foul off pitchers left and right to get a walk. What I couldn't understand about Stanky was if he had that kind of bat control to foul off pitchers, why wasn't he a better hitter when he swung the bat? He would deliberately foul off balls, punch a ball, bunt a foul, or whatever to run a count on that pitcher to get a walk. Stanky was not a naturally gifted ballplayer, but just an aggressive little fellow. Branch Rickey made the remark one time that he was the only player he ever saw that couldn't run, couldn't hit, and couldn't throw, but was a good ballplayer. Stanky was a kind of arrogant, cocky little fellow who didn't make too many friends, stayed to himself, and was always popping off in the clubhouse.

Dixie Walker was one of the most popular ballplayers that ever put a Dodgers uniform on. As anyone going back to that era knows, we had a real short fence at Ebbets Field, and Dixie could play that wall as well as anyone I have known. He would know exactly when a ball was going to hit that wall, which direction it was going to bounce, how many hops it was going to take, and he could have it back in the infield before you could turn around. In fact, a few times he tried to throw runners out at first base on a hard line drive hit there.

But Dixie made himself as popular as I can say. He made every event, every banquet, every outing, met with the people, went to kid programs, gave talks. He was an outstanding ballplayer as well, dedicated to his work. His brother Harry Walker played for the St. Louis Cardinals and was an exceptional ballplayer in his own right. Neither one of them had exceptional power, although Dixie was capable of hitting an occasional home run. They were more line-drivers, singles and doubles hitters who could get on base quite a bit.

There were some exceptional pitchers in the league at the time I played. Warren Spahn was at his peak and one of the better left-handers that ever put a uniform on; Howie Pollett was an exceptional pitcher. Both of them were control pitchers—"pitchers" not "throwers." They made every pitch have a purpose—they knew where they wanted to go with it, what they wanted to do with it.

The toughest pitcher I had to face when I got into the majors was a fellow named Ewell Blackwell. Ewell was about six foot six inches and 185 pounds—a real thin, slender, long-armed fellow that had a side-arm, crossfire delivery. He threw it almost three quarters underhanded and stepped out to throw it from third base. The first time I faced him was the first time I looked at a fastball and thought he had thrown a curve ball. With the velocity and angle that he threw it from, it would come up into your chest area and sink back away like a curve ball. He did have a curve ball and a slider and could throw hard. He could strike people out and he could win ballgames, but he eventually hurt his arm because he had such a slender shoulder and arm area that he damaged his muscles with that odd throwing motion.

Red Munger another pitcher, as hard a thrower as you could get, and they would run him in, and he could make it tough because brought fire with his fastball. Occasionally someone would say that he might wet it a little bit, but I never knew that for sure.

Negro League Legends

Even though I grew up in the segregated south, I have always had good black friends. The wife and I have never had any thoughts of racism. A human being is human being. I have quite a few black friends right here in Houston now, but there are two that should be recognized. One is Ralph Garr. Ralph played for the Atlanta Braves, was an outstanding ballplayer, and currently we go to the same church here in Houston.

Another great man is J. C. Hartman. J.C. played a year or two with the Houston Astros, but most of his career was in the Negro League. I have lunch with him and with Ralph often. We try to keep in touch and keep alive the memories from our era, like the time I faced Satchel Paige.

Satchel was one of the best-known black pitchers that ever came along, and he was quite a character as well. When I stepped in to face him for the first time, he leaned forward on his knee and glared toward the catcher to get his sign. Then he hesitated, looked up at me, and said, "Big man, I know what kind of pitches you like, but I'm telling you right now you ain't going to see none of them, so just make up your mind to that."

I had never had a pitcher talk to me before, so I stepped out of the batter's box and turned to the umpire. "Why is that man trying to talk to me?" He said there wasn't any rule against it, and he wasn't bothering anything and to just go along with it.

So I stepped back in. Satchel Paige ran a couple of pitches by me and ran up a count. Then he decided to break one of his curve balls in on my knee down low. Well, I was a low-ball hitter. I timed the thing and hit it completely out of the ballpark. As I began circling the bases I noticed that was watching me.

My next time at bat, Satchel leaned down in his position on his knee and said, "Now, big man, you know what you hit, you know where it was, and you know what kind of pitch it was, and I promise you'll never see that pitch again." And he was right—he moved that ball all around, up and down, this way and that, and I never did see it.

Stan the Man

Stan Musial stands out in my mind as one of the most down-to-earth, everyday, can-do-it-all type of ballplayer they had. There were some good ballplayers up there, but he was the most consistent and steady, no scandals, no loud mouthing, no nothing. He was just an ordinary, quiet, do-his-job type ballplayer. He could adjust himself to just about any situation when he came to bat; if he needed a single to drive in a run, you could see him adjust his stance and everything and just meet the ball for a single. If he thought a home run was necessary, or would help the cause at that time at bat, he would adjust himself a little differently and wait until he got his pitch and try to raise that ball up, and the majority of the time he could do it.

One particular ballgame, Marty Marion, "Mr. Short-stop," was playing shortstop and he hit ahead of Stan Musial. Well, Marty Marion was a real weak, what we called an "all-American-out" type of hitter, so he would work a walk to try to get on base. This particular time, he walked, he got on first base, and Stan Musial, coming up, was a left-hand hitter. Well, I get behind the runner—I don't hold him right on the bag because you kind of try to close the holdup with the left-hand hitter there—and I was standing about ten feet behind Marty Marion who was the runner on first, when Stan Musial gets the inside pitch he wants, and he drives a line drive at me.

I had never had one hit at me quite that hard, but when the ball is hit right at you, you stand still to catch it. But this thing had so much force on it, and he had driven it so hard, that the ball curved just like a pitcher's curve ball. Being left-handed, I had the glove on my right hand and that ball was curving toward the foul line, and I had to reach for it as fast as I could, a full arm stretch across my chest. When I finally caught the ball it had so much force it jerked my arm to where my shoulder and upper arm came in contact with my chin, and it even jolted my head and knocked my cap off. I ran over and tagged the base, and everyone started kidding me, saying, "Ed, you better be careful, that man's going to hurt you."

Well, we go on through the ballgame a little more, and the same situation comes up in a later inning. Marty Marion walks, gets on first base, Stan Musial's the batter, and I'm behind Marion to cover the hole. Same pitch, same situation, and he hits the next one a little harder right at me—a line drive that's curving to beat the daylights. I realized from that first one what it was going to do, so I braced myself for it, reached out full arm's length toward first base to head the curving ball off—and when I caught the ball my arms and shoulder flew up into my face and chin, knocked my cap off, and I had to go about two or three steps backwards from the force of it before I tagged the base again. I told Marty to tell Stan that that was enough of that—that he had tried me enough and to try somebody else.

Three Eddies

Back when I was a member of the Pittsburgh ball club, we had a left-hand pitcher, Bill Werle, who was a highly competitive left-hander, and he looked like he was almost going into convulsions with arm, legs, elbows, and leg kicks, and you never knew when he was turning the ball loose because of all the gyrations in his delivery. We were playing one particular ballgame, and Bill was pitching. At that time we had a catcher named Eddie Fitzgerald, a third baseman named Eddie Bochman, and of course myself at first base. During the course of the ballgame, a big right-hander came up there, and he got hold of a ball and hit a real high popup on the infield. So the catcher came out, I came out, and the third baseman came out. Usually when a pitcher sees who is closest to it and who is the best catcher, he will call their name out, and in this case Bill Werle looked it over and he said, "Eddie, you take the ball." Now three Eddies were trying to catch the ball, and of course we all ran together and dropped the ball, and the man was safe because Eddie was going to catch it, and each of the three of us thought it was our call.

Celebrities

I was a small-town boy, never had been anywhere and never had much to do in the ole world, but baseball took me to New York City with the Brooklyn Dodgers, where I met several celebrities. I found that not only were they celebrities, but they were fine people as well.

Bing Crosby, one of the Pittsburgh owners, was one of the most gentle, easygoing people you would ever want to meet, and when I told him I was born in Galveston, Texas, he started rattling off all the people he knew in Galveston. It was just like old home week! As I mentioned earlier, Bing would come in our clubhouse and put his uniform on, and even sing in our shower. He would bring his boys out to the ballpark, and I got acquainted with them. I've got a picture hanging on the wall now that pleases me no end: "To our good friend, Ed Stevens, from the Crosby boys."

Most of the famous folks I met were easy to talk to. Jack Benny traveled with us on one of our train trips once. While we were sitting in the Pullman car chatting, he said, "Ed, you know every time I come around a ball club in a big town, the newspapers all ask if I'm trying to buy a ball club. I'm not going to buy any ball club; I just enjoy baseball and meeting the ballplayers and baseball people."

Perry Como, Danny Kaye, George Raft, Eddie Arnold, and Harry James were all great people and performers, and I'll always cherish the time when I rubbed shoulders with celebrities.

Baseball Clowns

Baseball has always had what I call baseball clowns—fellows who would entertain the people before a ballgame or between double headers. Al Shack was into the big time, top hat and a tuxedo jacket over his uniform, and he did all kinds of things. When his time was through, ole Max Patkin came along, about a six foot five, loose-jointed fellow who could do everything in the world except turn himself inside out. He was really a fine comedian, and was one of the most popular clowns I have run across. And, of course, there was Jackie Price, a little small fellow who spent a little time in the big leagues. He could tie himself upside down and hit baseballs on a rack that was holding him up, and chase balls in a jeep. He could do all sorts of things that were very entertaining.

Rube Melton was a big rough-and-tough older pitcher who didn't like Durocher. One afternoon during our spring in Bear Mountain, Durocher was sitting in the lobby on a big couch wearing his pricy blue suede shoes. Well Rube decided to crawl under the couch and attach matches to Durocher's shoe soles. He lit the matches and somehow managed to get our of the lobby before it started burning Durocher's foot. Durocher was furious because it burned a hole in his blue suede shoes. He raised cane over the issue, cussing up a storm, but never found out who really did it.

Inflation

My first year in the big leagues, 1944, we had a young fellow named Tommy Brown, a young New York boy, who was making $250 a month playing major-league baseball. Another young player that ended up having a great career in the major leagues was Calvin McLish. When we all went to eat after a ballgame, he made an excuse and said he didn't want to go, and we kept picking at him until we found out that Calvin did not have enough money to eat on. Branch Rickey was paying him $150 to $175 a month.

My first year up from Triple A to the major leagues in 1945, I was paid $600 a month, and that was just for five months. I had to rush home to Galveston, Texas, as soon as the season was over and get myself a job as soon as I got there to pay my bills and get us through the winter and try to have enough money for the next spring training. You really had to fight heel and toe to get them to put it in your contract that they would pay your way to spring training and also give you money to get home on. If you didn't have that in your contract, you had to get home the best way you could.

Baseball has come a long way. We now have millionaire players. I don't begrudge them the money, but it hurts when you see the lack of dedication and loyalty. It's all greed now—who will pay the most. I was hurt when I had to leave the Dodgers because ballplayers back then didn't want to be traded—we loved the team we played for. But today's ballplayers are gone if someone else will give them a million dollars more.

Off-Season Odd Jobs

During the winters I did any number of odd jobs to make some money until ball season. I drove trucks, worked in foundries, and worked on the waterfront unloading big merchant marine ships. One of the jobs I will never forget was a prison guard. One of my brothers-in-law was a highway patrolman in Mississippi, and he told me that I could get some pretty good work at that City Prison Farm in Galveston. I had never been around prisoners, never had any experience. I talked to a fellow named Potts Johnson, a real nice man, and he said, "Ed, you come on down here, and I'll work you every winter."

I said, "Well, Captain, I don't know anything about handling prisoners or anything."

He said, "All we get out here is petty thieves, minor criminals, drunks, alcoholics, people who won't pay their tickets. Every once in a while we get a tough convict in, but it's no problem at all." So I decided to take the job.

I kept the name Big Ed Stevens. I was a pretty good-sized man—still muscular and heavy at that time. So I put the uniform on—we wore uniforms with badges and big ole cowboy hats—and I became a prison guard. Most of the guards were older men, and pretty much all they had ever done was work prison farms, and most of them just seemed to kind of hate the world, you might say. I spent most of my time trying to keep them from hurting some of the prisoners who didn't deserve to be hurt. With my size, I could stop a lot of the problems just by the fact that I looked big enough that no one wanted to find out if I was tough. I was tickled to death that they felt that way because I never prized myself as being a tough man, though I wouldn't back off if I had a problem.

So most of the time if they had a prisoner they couldn't handle they'd say to get Ed up here and he would talk to them. I was a pretty good talker, and I could reason with a man and calm him down without hurting anyone. Every so often we'd have a couple of guards that would really try to hurt some of those people, and I would jump in and pull him off of them and stop him from hitting them with a club or something. I kept peace out there pretty good, and in fact I think I gained the respect of most all the prisoners out there. I enjoyed working there, but like I say, every once in a while you would get a hardened criminal, I mean a convict in there, and you would kind of have to work around and work soft with him.

We fed them well and took care of them, but in this one particular case, I had a prisoner who was about forty years old and been in and out of jail most all his life. He gave me quite a bit of a problem there, and I had to discipline him—I didn't hurt him any, but I roughed him up enough to let him know that I was in charge and for him to settle down. Then I put him in a cell and locked him back up.

Well, when he got out of jail he called the captain and said, "I'm going on record right now that that Boss Stevens (they called us all boss) has roughed me up and embarrassed me to no end, and if I get a chance, I'm going to kill the man.

I've got me a gun, and I'll shoot him." The captain didn't tell me about it for about two and a half months, but when he did we decided we had to carry pistols. I made sure I had mine with me when I'd come out of the house to go to work and look all around for him.

I never told my wife that I had been threatened to be killed. He was just mean enough he could have done it if he decided to go through with it, but anyway for about two and a half months I was real cautious, watching everything I did, looking for him.

After two and a half months he showed up back in jail. Well, the captain hides him out, keeps him in a separate cell, and he told the rest of the guards, "Don't let Ed know we have this man back. I don't want him to confront him." Well, when it came time to feed them, they let everybody out, and I noticed that the guard told one fellow not to come out, so I went on with the feeding, giving them their lunch, and all at once it dawned on me.

I said, "What was wrong with that fellow back there that you wouldn't let out?"

He said, "Ed, I'm not supposed to tell you this, but that was the fellow who said that he was going to shoot you."

I said, "Oh my goodness!" So I made up a tray of food, took it back there and unlocked the door, and I said, "I understand you've been looking for me."

He said, "Oh boss, nuh uh, not me. I—I didn't do nothing like that."

So I put the tray down and told him I had brought him some food. We carried a big ring of brass keys to open all those big iron doors—had about seven or eight keys on it. So I threw it up on the bed where he was standing, and I told him to take the keys, and I would let him use it as a weapon. That I wasn't going to use anything, but that we would find out how tough he was and who he wanted to kill.

He said, "Boss, please, I don't want no trouble with you. I apologize for saying that, and I never had no intention of doing that." I grabbed him by the shirt and shook him up and told him that I ought to beat the living daylights out of him, but it wasn't my nature. I wasn't going to hurt him, but that I thought he and I had to have an understanding from now on. He said, "Boss, you got that, I'll never do anything like that again." That ended that, but just not knowing if a man is serious about shooting you, that shook me up a little bit.

Warren Spahn's Low Ball

One other especially proud memory of mine is of Warren Spahn, the left-handed pitcher with the Boston Braves who was one of the top left-handers in baseball. When I got into the major leagues with Brooklyn and especially over at Pittsburgh, Warren Spahn's type of pitching was very controlled—he knew where he wanted the ball to go, he kept it off the edge of the plate, he could move it up and down and change speeds, just an exceptional pitcher. When we were both through with our playing careers he paid me one of the finest compliments I could receive as a hitter in major-league baseball.

He was managing Tulsa in the American Association Triple A baseball. I was scouting for the Minnesota Twins at that time, and we would all get together after a ballgame and have a little snack and bull sessions up in the press room. He took me aside and told me that he wanted to ask me something. He said he had been able to get out just about anybody in the National League, and he wanted to know what he had been doing differently with me that I could hit him so well. He said that everything he threw I hit home runs or extra base hits and that he had gone home and told his wife that Pittsburgh had a young superstar in the making over there, Ed Stevens.

I said, "Warren, I can put it this way. You were an exceptional control pitcher, and you always used your theory of pitching low. I knew that you had perfect control and that you pitched low, that you threw straight overhand. And even though your ball was moving and you had good stuff on it, I was a low inside ball hitter, that's where all my power came from."

He said, "So now you tell me!"

Growing up in Galveston

My mother was from Mississippi and my daddy was from Kentucky. They settled in Galveston and raised four of us boys: Harold, the oldest, Malcolm next, myself, and my brother Gerald, who was a lot younger. I never dwell on things like this, but fact was we were a very disorganized family. My poor ole daddy never got a dollar ahead, just worked for the railroad barely scratching out a living. There was no religion or church life. My brother Malcolm, who was about three years older than I was, started playing baseball before me, and I was playing American Legion ball at thirteen. Most of the townspeople said that Malcolm was going to be the ballplayer in the family, and that Eddie would never make it because he wasn't as good as his brother.

The townspeople all said that a Galveston boy never went anywhere and never did any good. My brothers would never take any time with me, and I was meek and had a lacked confidence. It was tough to gain the confidence in myself to try and go play baseball, because I was running scared twenty-four hours a day from lack of maturity and no family guidance to amount to anything.

Soon Malcolm moved up a little bit in pro ball. I mentioned earlier that he said, "Eddie, when you learn how to hit, you can go play ball." I appreciated him saying that, and I worked on it, but what it boiled down to, again, was that Malcolm was going to be the big boy in the family, and Eddie was just going to bring up the rear. I was never going to amount to what Malcolm did. My little ole mother, as far as I'm concerned and the rest of us realized, she only had one son, and that was Malcolm. My poor ole mother threw everything into Malcolm.

When I started playing ball, trying to gain maturity, the thing that kept me going in my career was God-given ability to play baseball. I had a natural talent, and I was working as hard as I could to develop it, sharpen what talent I had, put an edge on it. I eventually started moving ahead of my brother. The townspeople continued their nay saying, "Well, he isn't going to make it—Malcolm is still going to outdo Eddie. He can't play ball like Malcolm does."

Malcolm got as high as AA baseball and never got any further. And little by little I moved from class D up through the ranks. In 1944 I went to spring training in a Dodger camp and made the AAA ball club. My ability was starting to stand out, and a manager, Bruno Betzel, took a liking to me and took me with him to Montreal. As time went on, even my other brothers were saying that Eddie got all the breaks, and Malcolm didn't get any. This was the reason he wasn't doing better than Eddie.

I never tried to fight that situation; I was family, but the idea was that I was second in the family and wasn't going to amount to anything and that my brother Malcolm was going to do it all. Malcolm could hit a baseball; he could hit just about anybody who picked up a ball and threw it at him, but unfortunately he didn't have much running speed, he didn't have a throwing arm, and he was just a mediocre fielder. In fact, during that time he was what they called a "one-tool" ballplayer. What I mean by that is he could only hit and couldn't do anything else. You didn't move up the ladder in ball playing just being a one-tool player. You had to hit, be an adequate fielder, and run a little to move on.

I started developing those things and moved on and, of course, eventually achieved my dream. Not many people had confidence in me. I had to build my own. I had to push like the devil to get a little maturity. During the Durocher days, due to my lack of maturity and running scared, Durocher almost crushed my life. But I kept pecking away in spite of him and, of course, eventually made it to the big leagues.

From then on, everything kind of quieted down a little bit around home and my family life settled down some. After Malcolm had played awhile, he got himself married and had a real beautiful little girl and was madly in love with her. Unfortunately it didn't work out for them, and the next I knew my brother had started hitting the bottle. He became a drinking man, a bar-room brawler, getting himself thrown in jail and embarrassing us every time we turned around.

Of course, my having a halfway decent name in the family, I was always called to try to smooth everything out, get him out of jail and help. When my brother was sober, he bragged on me for all it was worth and tell everyone that brother of his was really doing some good. But when he would get a few drinks in him, he would start belittling me and even have some of his bar-room friends call me up and make insulting remarks. He resented the fact that I made the major leagues and he didn't.

Milk Ball

I mentioned earlier that we were from a very poor neighborhood with a lot of blacks and a lot of Mexican boys and a few white people, and we all got along. Nobody had any money, but we didn't let that bother us. Since we couldn't buy bats or balls or that sort of thing, we would round up in the neighborhood and get all the Carnation milk cans we could find. Then we'd find old worn-out broomsticks and take the straw off them to make bats.

We would wait until night, because we had awfully hot summers down in the southern part of Texas. We would get out under the lights and play ball with our piecemeal gear. Over time the tin was winning the battle because it was chewing up all of our wooden broomsticks, so we would have to shut down and hunt the neighborhood for more broomsticks to keep our bats going. That was how we entertained ourselves before the modern equipment, the playing fields, and the uniforms, and I'm proud that things have progressed that much. We didn't have any high school ball when I was coming along, and the best thing we could do was to play "Sandlot," American Legion, and amateur ball. Whatever it took, we would ride our bicycles and round up players to play a game.

Our Major League Bat

There were no washing machines when I was growing up, and my mother and all the other mothers and grandmothers had to wash on what they called "scrub boards." Octagon was a real strong popular soap that everyone used for washing clothes, and my mother would buy four or five bars of it at a time and wash the clothes with that scrub board.

Octagon soap had coupons in every one of their soap bars so that you could collect them and if you got enough of them you could get a professional baseball bat. My brothers and I scanned the neighborhood and insisted on our mother buying all the soap she could get. It took up a while to get enough coupons for a bat, but when we finally counted them out, we realized that we finally had enough of them. We all went down to the store, and they looked the coupons over and said, "That's right. You're earned a major-league baseball bat."

We took that thing home just as proud as we could be—each one of us taking a turn holding it, and it wasn't any time at all until we got out in a little sandlot and we were going to try out our major-league bat. That was unheard of in our neighborhood.

My oldest brother, Harold, was the oldest so he got to try the bat out first, and I was throwing the batting practice. I wasn't very big, but I could throw fairly well. I threw him a good straight ball and he laid into it, and when the bat made contact it shattered into four pieces. We all gathered and stared at the bat laying all over the ground. We had never been so disappointed—on the first pitch.

Baseball Wives

Back in our playing days, a baseball wife had to be a special woman who loved baseball and would back her husband completely in the career that he was following. During our time, wives and families were not allowed to come with their husbands to spring training, and in most of our cases, the wives and children had to stay home until spring training broke. Wives and children had to stay home until we could see what town we would end up playing in.

My wife, Margie, whom I married back in 1943, was one of those devoted, dedicated baseball players' wives, and I admire and appreciate her a great deal for it. If I was playing in Brooklyn, New York, Margie would load up our three daughters in Galveston, Texas, and drive all the way to Brooklyn, find us an apartment before the Dodgers got back in town, and be already set up in an apartment before I ever got there.

The expense of getting our families to the town where we were playing was all our own. She even drove to Toronto, Canada, with the children all by herself, and to Indianapolis, Indiana. In one particular case, when she got to Indianapolis, I was in training with the Cleveland organization with the Indianapolis ballclub, and that's when I was traded over to Toronto in the international league. Well, Margie hadn't had any word of this and she drove all the way to Indianapolis and called the ballpark.

Back then, a lot of the people in the town would rent

their houses furnished to ballplayers for the summer so they could go to their summer homes and make a little extra money. So she called the Indianapolis ballpark and asked for some apartment information and the front office person she talked to didn't know how to handle it or what to do. He told her that he hated to be the one to tell her this because he knew she had come all the way to Indianapolis from Texas, but her husband had been sold to Toronto. She told him that she hadn't realized that, and she thanked him.

She was staying with a little family we had stayed with the year before, and she got out her road map to figure out how to get to Toronto, Canada, from Indianapolis. She loaded those kids up and drove from Indianapolis, Indiana, to Toronto, Canada, where the snow was still on the ground. The Canadian teams had to open their season on the road, and we were on the road about ten days before we could get back to Toronto, our home base. So she was in a motel when we got there, and by then, the snow had left so we were able to use the playing fields. We stayed in this motel about two weeks until we found an apartment, and Margie never let out a whimper or got disgusted with anything because she knew that was our living, that was our life, and those little girls just went right along with it; in fact they thought it was exciting for them to move around and be in different towns.

I know of several ballplayers who had wives who did not want their husbands playing baseball, they hated it and didn't want to be home alone while he was gone, and some of the players just had to give up and quit. Fortunately I had a wife that backed me 100%, helped me through all my trials and tribulations, through my good days and my bad. Of course today wives can go on road trips with the ballclub on their chartered airplanes.

We never thought a thing about it because that was the way of life and what you had to do, so I will always admire and respect Margie for standing behind me—in fact, she's still behind me. Even during my twenty-nine years of scouting when I was gone two and three weeks at a time. She always had to be the mom, the dad, the caretaker, and the doctor.

Thoughts on the Modern Game

Baseball was baseball back in those days! If you faltered the least bit, you were back in the minor leagues because they had ballplayers playing all over the country, and every year that I played I had to battle with five or six first basemen in the spring to end up on the big club. At that time, it was either the Dodgers or the Pirates for me. I've said this earlier in some of my remarks, but I would give anything if they played it like baseball was played in the 20s, 30s, 40s, and 50s. Today there is too much greed, no loyalty, no dedication—just where the money goes, that's where they go. Of course I would have loved to have made some money, but I was pleased and proud to play for the club I was playing for, and it never crossed my mind to even try to go to another club. Of course, that program wasn't even in when I was playing, and it was so easy to be sent to the minor leagues because there were so many players around. You just played your heart out and tried to stay with the big club as best you could, and if you got back to AAA, you battled your way to try to get back on another big club or the club you left.

Baseball has changed a great deal, and today I don't really know where to put my finger on it, but I have never seen so many homeruns hit in my life. My first thought was that maybe the ball was all juiced up to go a lot farther than it did years ago, but I really and truly think the caliber of major-league pitching has fallen off a great deal. In fact, very few clubs have real top-notch, front-line major-league pitchers on their club. They run in a lot of relievers and their fourth and fifth starters who don't seem to have the demanding stuff to hold the club back or be tough in their pitching. My feeling right now is that the homeruns come from inferior pitching.

Your top-notch pitcher is not a "thrower," he's a "pitcher." A *thrower* just throws the ball somewhere near home plate, but a *pitcher* has direction, purpose, and will make it his business to not throw a perfect strike. He'll try to make you swing at a bad ball, he'll try to make you swing in the dirt, or chase a high pitch, or hit you on the fist with an inside pitch. My explanation of a *thrower* is one who just rears back and throws at home plate with no idea where he wants to go with it, and I believe that's where a lot of them get in trouble.

But baseball is still being played today, and though I can find a few faults with the modern players and management, they are keeping the game going, and I'm proud for that. I hope one of these days it will all level off and get back to the point to where loyalty and dedication mean a lot more than switching clubs and jumping around for the bigger money.

Slump

I have been asked about slumps many times. The question goes something like this: How does it happen that a player who's making good contact at the plate, getting extra base hits, driving in runs, and it seems like you're never going to get him out, and suddenly he walks up there and can't meet the ball properly and loses sight of the strike zone. This is what baseball calls a "slump."

A slump begins when your hitting falls off and you just can't get a rhythm going, and then it's compounded as tension and stress set in when you begin to press. It also affects your swing; you just lose track of the strike zone and you're swinging at bad balls, you're leaning out on the front foot, and you're doing everything you weren't doing when you were hitting that well.

My advice for getting out of a slump is to concentrate more, but not stress and strain, because the more you push yourself, the farther you get away from it. I've been in slumps, and some of them lasted a pretty good while, but in time I learned that when the pitcher starts his windup, the average hitter will lean forward on his front foot, which you should not do because when you get out on your front foot, all you have left is an arm swing.

Instead, if you drop back on your back foot, get all your weight back there, and then come forward, that will eliminate stepping out a little too quick and leaning toward the pitcher. Hitting is about balance, concentration, and determination, having confidence in yourself that you can get it all back. It is a struggle to get through that, but I've seen a lot of hitters that just push themselves in the wrong ways.

Thoughts on the Modern Game/Techniques

Today's ballplayers do some strange things, especially the first basemen. I played first base all my life and earned a pretty good reputation for making all my plays and handling the bag properly. The majority of the players these days play a stationary first base. When the ball is thrown from the infield— short, second, third—today's first baseman will plant his foot on the bag and wait for the throw. Well, I believe that if your foot is placed on the bag, you don't have the agility to move to the left or to the right. I was taught to run over, touch the bag with your heel to know where it is at, and then straddle the base a little bit and wait to see where the throw is going to be—then you could move into that position with a shift and tag it. If it's to the left, you tag it with your right foot, if it's on the right side of the bag, you tag it with your left, and that way you're more agile and can play it.

And on low throws, how many times have you seen the modern-day first baseman slap at a ball in the dirt rather than get down with it? I would always drop down on one knee and get level with the ball, and then I could see what it was doing, and very few balls ever got through me. A lot of your first basemen are a little uneasy about a hard-thrown ball that's going to bounce, and they don't know how high or where it's going to go.

Of course I'm not putting any of them down because they're still playing in the big leagues; they just don't play it the way we were taught when we were coming up, back in what people refer to as "when baseball was baseball." I don't like to put down the present-day ballplayers, but it's so different from when I played in the 40s and 50s and 60s, and like I say, I mentioned earlier there's no loyalty, no discipline, and all greed—give me the money, and I'll play for you! Back then we were tickled to death to stay with one club.

One of my favorite modern first basemen was Will Clark, who played for the Giants all those years. He had the knack of shifting and handling that bag, and going down for the low throws. Another was Keith Hernandez, who played for the Cardinals, and he was another smooth fielder. If you've got the agility to move with the ball, get in front of it, backhand it, or whatever it takes, but stay with the ball and not grab at it, you do a lot better. Another good one was Raphael Palmeiro. He was as smooth and as sure of a first baseman as you could play it. Those three stand out in my mind as people who could play the bag like it ought to be played.

Scouting: Throwers vs. Pitchers

My scouting years began in 1962 and lasted until 1989. That's twenty-nine years of scouting American Legion, amateur, junior colleges, four-year colleges, universities, the pro leagues, the major leagues, and the minor leagues, quite a bit of coverage in scouting for one man. I covered five states during my scouting career including Texas, Louisiana, Oklahoma, and Arkansas. There were times when I would scout a double-header in one town and have to drive several hours to get close enough to the next town in order to spend the night so I would be in town the next day for the ballgame.

Scouting was very exciting, and during that era, '62 to '89, I previewed some of the most well known ballplayers today. My list starts with Nolan Ryan.

He was a young boy in high school in Alvin, Texas, a small town about twenty miles from Houston, and when I first picked up on Nolan Ryan, he was as skinny as a bedrail, had what we call a sunken chest, and was just as frail-looking as could be, but he showed good arm action, and a loose, free delivery. Of course he didn't start throwing the speed and the stuff he had after he became a professional until he got stronger, filled out, and got bigger.

Nolan was drafted by the New York Mets, and he had quite a time over there because he could throw hard but had no idea about strike zones. He was so wild that the Mets gave up on him and traded him off because they didn't think he would ever get enough control and learn the fundamentals of strike zone and how to pitch to hitters, He was traded to the Angels and was still having a control problem, but when he was traded to the Houston Astros and had quite a few years there he began his big strike-out career, because he was striking out people along the way, and he had finally gotten enough control that he cold stay in the ballgame and hold people off and do his thing.

Nolan Ryan is what I would call, and this is no put-down to him, a "thrower"; in other words, he just threw the ball somewhere toward home plate hoping that it would be enough for a strike or be a strike. Your control pitcher is what I call a "pitcher"; he has his spots picked out, and he has massive control of his pitches. Nolan would never throw a good strike. He would throw the ball inside, outside, up a little bit, or just off the center of the plate, never throwing a good pitch to be hit. That was one of his problems. He had such tremendous speed and a strong arm, he tried his best to see how many people he could strike out and, of course, he had a pretty career doing it, but I'm sure he could have done a lot better if he had gone for spot pitching, going for the double play instead of just throwing the ball by everybody. All that said, my hat's off to Nolan Ryan with the career he had.

My next man would be Roger Clemens. Roger is right out of a suburb of Houston called Katy, Texas. I scouted Roger in high school, San Jacinto Junior College and at the University of Texas in Austin. Roger Clemens, even in his college days, could throw hard, but had no command of his pitches, didn't have much of a breaking ball, and his fastball didn't move that much. Even though he could throw hard, he really didn't take command out there like a pitcher should.

He was drafted by the Boston Red Sox. Now when I say drafted, at the time when I first started scouting, there was no such thing as the draft like they have now. You could go in and sign a ballplayer regardless of your finish in the league. You were just fighting off your competition and hoping you could sell the boy on signing. But when the draft came in, the last-place club would get first shot, the next-to-last place would get the next shot, and so on. Some of the names I'm mentioning here I had in as top prospects, but if your draft number didn't come up and somebody drafted them ahead of you, you didn't have a shot. And so the Red Sox drafted Roger Clemens.

Now Roger was, as I said, just an ordinary hard thrower in college, but I ran into him again in AA baseball in the Red Sox organization. I was scouting the league he was in, and when he took the mound, I could see all the difference in the world. Roger was throwing a real short breaking ball, a slider that could get anybody out, and his fastball was starting to move. That was when I realized Roger had really found himself as a major-league pitcher. He could hit his spots and would throw off-speed stuff, never a perfect strike, but close enough to have you take a swing at it.

Both of these gentlemen will be in the Hall of Fame, and I'm proud that I was able to scout them and witness their careers from early on.

David Clyde was an eighteen-year-old boy right out of Westchester High School here in the city of Houston. The young man was about six foot one, 180 pounds, had the best pitching rhythm, had a major-league fastball, could roll a curve off a table, and you couldn't see anything to improve in the boy even though he was a high school pitcher.

David was highly sought after, and of course I turned him in as a top prospect to the club I was scouting for, the Minnesota Twins. But unfortunately he was drafted by the Texas Rangers before my club could get a shot at him.

David Clyde went right from high school to the Texas Rangers in the American League in Arlington, Texas. Minnesota was the first club he faced. They packed that stadium. They glorified him and praised him to the high heavens, and he was a drawing card from the word go. Of course, the Minnesota players said, "Ed, you scouted him. Tell us something about him." I told them that David threw hard, he had good control, his ball had good movement, he had a short-breaking curve ball, and he would throw strikes. He'd be right around that plate. Well, he mowed down the Minnesota Twins just like an established ballplayer, and that really established him.

They started using him with the Rangers as a drawing card, and I remember in some of his starts, they would hold the ballgame back until more fans got in the ballpark to see him pitch. Billy Martin was the manager over there at that time, and I really believe, with all due respect because Billy Martin is no longer with us, but from what I could see of it, Billy was taking advantage of that young man, pitching him way too often to try to win more games, draw people in the ballpark, and, of course, he eventually hurt his arm up around the shoulder area and never did bounce back. He's still living here in Houston, and I wish him all the best. I'm proud of that young man, and his is just one of the many young careers that got sidetracked because of injury.

Another man I scouted was Doug Draybeck, who pitched for Rice University, went to the Pittsburgh Pirates. You could see in college that Draybeck, a strong right-hander who had control of all his pitches, knew how to pitch, knew how to move the ball, and had pitching knowledge. He went on and had some great years with my old Pittsburgh ball club.

Rick Honeycutt also pitched for the Pittsburgh Pirates organization with their AA club. On this night, he was scheduled to pitch in Tulsa, Oklahoma. Rick had been offered to Seattle as part of a deal; he was to be one of the players Pittsburgh would give up if they could make the deal. My general manager got hold of me and told me to "get in there" because we needed a left-handed pitcher. He told me to call him in his office as soon as I had seen him to decide whether or not to bring him up.

Some of the other scouts felt I would be wasting my time and that he wasn't a good ballplayer. They said that he couldn't pitch or throw hard enough, and they didn't think I would like him. I saw Rick pitch that night anyway, and he showed me that he had control of his pitches, he had pitching knowledge, he moved the ball around, changed speeds, kept it out of the strike zone, and made the batters hit his pitches—bad balls off the plate.

I got on the phone and called my man and told him, "Look, you get him up there just as quick as you can, start him on the road somewhere so he can get his confidence, and you've got yourself a big-league pitcher." Some of the players that night asked me how I could recommend Rick Honeycutt—they hadn't seen him do anything. I told them to just wait and see, because I saw a major leaguer.

Rick had himself a tremendous career for several franchises and then went on to do some TV work. I was proud to play a role in his journey to the big leagues.

Scouting: Clark, Palmeiro, and Garr

Will Clark and Raphael Palmeiro were both student-athletes at Mississippi State at the same time. They were both first basemen, but Will Clark was elected to play first, and Palmeiro agreed to play the outfield so they could both make the lineup. Both were left handed, and you could see watching the two boys hit that they were definite big-league material. They both had a good approach to hitting, would just walk in there and drive the ball all over the place.

When I'd seen enough, I took our scouting director with me to watch these boys and to okay the ballplayers and help me put them on the draft list. In the ballgame we watched, Will Clark hit the ball real well, and I had already seen Palmeiro hit before I ever brought the man down, so I knew they were both exceptional hitters. But when the scouting director saw them both play, he told me that he would like Will Clark, but he didn't want anything to do with Palmeiro.

I said, "You're my boss, and I work for you, and I'll honor anything you say, but I want you to put me on record that Palmeiro is going to be as good a player as Clark or better. They will both be outstanding major-league ballplayers." He wouldn't buy that and said that he would turn Will Clark in, but not Palmeiro. The draft had a lot to do with it, but in this case my scouting director didn't like two major-league prospects on the same club. But that happens.

Now we are going to talk about Ralph Garr, a black ballplayer. I scouted him at Grambling University, in Grambling, Louisiana. Ralph was playing second base, and he had exceptional speed. He was a left-hand hitter and had a knack for making contact and getting on base. Ralph didn't have the smooth motions that most ballplayers have, some of his were awkward moves, but he could still get the work done.

One of the things I noticed right away about Ralph— the thing that Pee Wee Reese taught me when I was with the Dodgers—was that when a ground ball was hit, Ralph put his glove down on the ground because if the ball came up, he could come up quicker than he could go down. I remember in one ballgame a ball was hit between first and second bases, and Ralph went after that thing with his glove on the ground, and those fingers were digging up dirt just like he was plowing up ground because he was told to keep that glove on the ground.

Ralph ended up with the Atlanta Braves playing outfield, where he broke some records that a lot of people respected, and still do. He lives here in Houston and is a real close friend of mine. He's still scouting for the Atlanta Braves. I appreciated Ralph as a ballplayer and as a personal friend.

Scouting: Stories from the Road

My last year as a scout was 1989. I have a lifetime gold pass to any ball club in the United States, and I go out and watch the Astros every now and again my grandsons. On those days I tend to miss the Astrodome; it takes a lot more work to get to their new ballpark downtown.

Scouting has changed almost as much as the game. When I scouted, $100,000 was a tremendous price. If you gave a boy $100,000 to sign with your ball club, you had better believe that boy could do something because you were putting your name on the line for that him to, hopefully, become a major-league ballplayer. That's peanuts nowadays; Lance Berkman, who played for Rice University here in Houston, was given $1 million by the Astros to sign a contract.

Our selling point was that although we weren't going to sign them as millionaires, we were signing them to become millionaires; they could make the big money when they got up into the big leagues. The process was pretty straightforward. I would see a boy one time, and if I liked some of the things he was doing, I'd go back two or three more times to see if he could continue to impress me. If he impressed me enough, I would stay with him and put him down and do everything I could do to get him drafted into my organization.

The first year I scouted, 1962, there was no draft, and I was fortunate enough to get my number one—Paul Ratliff, the left-handed hitting catcher—for the Minnesota Twins. At that time all of your scouts were former ballplayers that had worn the uniform and played professional ball, most of them in the major leagues, and they knew how it worked. My being a young scout, it took a little while to be accepted by the older scouts. They were jealous that I had landed Ratliff so early in my career, and I took a lot of remarks, as they were all wondering how a young punk scout like myself could do that.

I'd had to sell myself to him and to Paul and his family, because back then if the family you were talking to was impressed with the scout, they thought he was with a pretty good organization. I was honest and down to earth, and my approach resonated with the family from the get-go. And evidently I impressed those folks enough; of all the ball clubs that went after him, Paul decided to sign with Minnesota. Paul had a temper that got him in trouble sometimes, but he put in some good years with the club before traded over to Kansas City. He was my first major league recruit.

The older scouts didn't fool around much; they knew where they were going, what they wanted to do, and who they wanted to look at. No one ever gave their true opinions of the ballplayers because even though we were friends, running together and eating together, we were still competitors and we did our best to hide our feelings on our top prospects.

When I was scouting, I traveled in five states. There were times when I traveled so much and spent the night in so many hotels and motels that I had to get up in the morning and look at some stationery or a pack of matches to see what town I was in. A lot of times when we had a big tournament, all the scouts were in the same town, and we would all stay at the same motel.

There were a couple of older scouts who had what they called a "Hobo lunch"—they would go out and buy Vienna sausage, bread, mustard, bologna, enough to make sandwiches, and we'd drink a little beer and just sit around and have bull sessions to pass the time. We would discuss the tournament or the club we were looking at, but like I said, no one ever said anything to indicate how much interest he had in a particular boy. Each man had to decide for himself what he thought of that ballplayer. We were always a little cautious with each other, but we had some fun times.

One of the hairiest moments in my life happened on the scouting trail. We were in Oklahoma City scouting a big tournament and two of us, Red Gaskill of the Cleveland Indians and I, got back to the hotel about the same time. So we were waiting for all the other scouts to come in, and it was in between winter cutting out and summer starting, so they didn't have any heat or air on and it was a little warm in our hotel room.

I cracked the door a little to let some air in, and as we looked up all we saw was a gun barrel. A great big ole colt .45 pointed through that door, and behind it was a black man with one of those seaman's caps pulled down over his ears and sunglasses on. He was in the room with that gun on us, and he said, "This is a holdup. I want both of you men to get down on the floor and stay there."

You'd think we were in a ten-foot water pool the way we got down on that floor. When we got down there, he said, "I want all of your money, get your wallets out. I want your watches, your rings, everything you got I want."

Well, Red, trying to be a diplomat, told the man, "Look, don't take everything out of my wallet. I need a lot of those papers, driver's license, and everything."

That ole boy put the gun behind Red's head and said, "Just lie there and *shut up!* No talking!"

I reached over and grabbed Red by the arm and said, "Red, let's don't talk anymore. Let's do what the man says." So I ended up giving him what was in my wallet, a little pocket clip of bills, my watch, and he just cleaned us out. Red was still trying to talk to him, and I really thought he was going to get himself shot.

Just before he went out the door, he said, "If you get up and try to see which way I went, I'm going to shoot at you, and hope I hit you because you ain't going to see which way I'm going."

He went on out the door, and Red and I looked at each other. "Ed, you think we ought to get up?"

"Let's give him plenty of time to get where he's going," I said. "Let's just lay here and talk a little bit."

That was the last time I wanted to see any gunplay, so we stayed there long enough to make sure he was gone and got up reported it to the motel.

The police came out and investigated, asked us all kind of questions. One of the detectives said, "I'm gonna tell you why these people rob motels. Both of you fellows are from out of town, right?"

I said, "Oh, yeah, we're from Texas."

He said that the reason these holdups happened in motels was because the criminals knew that if they held you up you wouldn't bother coming back to file charges even if they were caught.

Word got all over the scouting world that Ed Stevens and Red Gaskill got themselves robbed in a motel in Oklahoma City. Everyone kidded us and wanted to know how big the gun was. We'd always say he rolled it in on wheels. Fortunately no one was hurt so we could make a joke out of it, but Red and I would always remember that night.

As my scouting career moved on, I noticed that baseball started getting away from professional baseball scouts and going with college boys, friends of friends, and people with no scouting and little baseball experience. I would see about five or six of them sitting all shoulder to shoulder looking at a pitcher and trying to decide if it was an average fastball or good speed. Was that a curve or a slider? I got a kick out of their inexperience, because the club would have to send a full-fledged established scout in to verify some of the things these younger boys were reporting.

The last few years I scouted, these young men were really lowering the standards of scouting. They started coming to the ballpark wearing tee shirts, no socks, chewing tobacco and spitting all over everything. Scouts, myself included, had traditionally worn clean clothes and dressed well. Quite a few of the scouts wore shirts and ties, and jackets unless it was really hot out. It was depressing to see the way scouting had turned to young inexperienced people. But the economics of the thing—the fact that they could hire these young boys a lot cheaper than they could an older scout—was the issue. Unfortunately, they weren't getting quality scouting.

Again, I'm proud of my era, and like I said, I'm sorry to see the scouting end of it depreciate. It's like baseball: I feel like baseball is not played like it was in my days, but it is still being played, and that's the big thing.

We scouts were all friends although we worked for different ball clubs and we were trying our best to get the pick of the best ballplayers around. Every so often one of us would get the word on some kid that none of the rest of the scouts knew anything about. When this happened to me, I would slip away from the back and ease over to where that boy was playing to see if we had a hidden prospect there before the rest of the group knew anything about it.

Sometimes that worked, and they didn't know about this young man, and sometimes he would be a fair ballplayer and sometimes he wouldn't be. But other times, when that scout would slip off thinking he had one hidden out, he would arrive at the ballpark only to find six other scouts there for this boy that "nobody knew anything about." I don't guess there is any such thing as hiding one out, but we tried.

For twenty-nine years I fortunate enough to experience just about everything that went on in the scouting business.

Family

God has blessed me with a wife and children. It was a rough-and-tumble road for me to become a ballplayer, but what turned my life around completely was a little lady, Margie Saxon, from Meadville, Mississippi. She grew up with a first cousin of mine. They were girlfriends together, and my cousin introduced me to Margie. We eventually got married when I was eighteen and she was seventeen years old, and the little girl just turned my life around.

We had three daughters, we started a church life; I started believing in and worshiping God. She was such an incredible influence on me and I feel very mature and comfortable in life now. We've been married sixty-six years now, so evidently our marriage took just like a vaccination "took." I'm proud of her and always will be.

We lost two daughters recently. Our oldest daughter, Janice, passed away at fifty-three, and our next to the oldest daughter had a serious case of diabetes, lost both of her feet, and was finally taken by the diabetes at fifty-two. Our love for them goes on.

Our youngest daughter, Vicki Lynn, is fifty-five today, and we are very proud of her. She is a highly religious young lady who has raised a beautiful family. She is well respected in her church life and all her children are God-fearing people. She's also a very talented young lady. She's a self-taught singer who has never had a lesson and can't read a note. She learns all of her songs, especially religious songs, and sings them at funerals, women's retreats, and church services. She has been to our church here in Houston, Westbury Baptist, four times putting on concerts, singing, and giving testimonies. She is our only daughter left, and she has been a solid rock for Margie and I to fall back on after the loss of our other two daughters.

We're still living here in Houston, happy and retired, grateful for the life we've had, hopeful that God will grant us many more years.

Malcolm passed away several years ago, and my younger brother, Gerald, was seventy-six when he passed away. I'm eighty-four at this time and still going. I'm proud of all my family members, my wife, our daughters living and passed on, our son-in-law, and all of our grandchildren and their families.

PHOTOGRAPHS

Ed during his Toronto days. He was popular for his southern accent and it played well with the western theme the radio station had. He commanded a 51% share of the 6 station listening area.

Approximately 1953

This is the family during spring training while at the Toronto club. In the picture from left to right are my wife, Margie, oldest daughter Janice, youngest daughter Vicki, myself, and middle daughter Barbara. We had spring training in Ft. Pierce Florida. Approximately 1955.

ACTION SHOT IN HISTORIC 1946 PLAYOFF between Dodgers and Cardinals. Stan Musical has just completed a great throw to pitcher Murry Dickson to retire Ed Stevens, Brooklyn first sacker, in second game, in Brooklyn.

Pictured left to right – Ed Stevens, Howie Schultz, Clyde Sukforth, Jackie Robinson, Jake Pitler, Ray Blades. Pregame picture in dug out in 1946, Ebbetts Field.

Ed Stevens and his brother Malcolm. Spring trained together in Bear Mountain New York 1945.

Action picture the first time Ed and Pittsburgh faced off against the Dodgers. Ed is sliding into Jackie trying to break up the double play. The slide was a little late but he still broke Jackie's action.

Jackie during the 1947 season. Pre game shot.

Ed and Bing Crosby. Bing was a part owner of the Pirates. This was in the club house of the Hollywood, Ca. spring training facility.

One of my prized pictures – a beautiful picture of one of the most popular ballparks in the country ... Ebbetts Field.

Me signing the first player I ever signed in my scouting career. His name is Paul Ratlif and he was the number one draft choice for Minnesota in 1962. Back in the day when a scout had to sell himself and the ball club to get the best players. No multi million dollar bonuses here.

Ralph Kiner – personal friend and outstanding home run hitter.

1941 Big Spring Bombers. My first year in professional baseball as a 16 year old! I'm the 8th player from the left.

In Toronto, being awarded a huge billboard after being voted as an allstar first baseman in the International League. Accompanying me in the picture is one of the team officials.

From left to right – Howie Schultz, Ed Stevens, Hall of Famer Dick Sisler, Jakie Robinson and Tommy Brown.

1946 starting infield for Brooklyn. From left to right, Pee Wee Reese, Ed Stevens, Cookie Lavigatta, Howie Schultz, Eddie Stanky, Augie Galan.

Me and Burley Grimes, who was the manager of the Toronto ball club. The hug was for the walk off home run I gave him a few minutes earlier. He was a hall of fame spit ball pitcher.

From left to right - Dixie Walker, Wally Westlake, Danny Murtaugh, Ralph Kiner, Ed Stevens. Dixie was celebrating the birth of his son. Spring training of 1948.

All time favorite baseball comedian. He was famous for performing comedy before the games and was a fan favorite. He would travel to all the ball clubs. This was during my National League days.

Opening day line up of infielders for Brooklyn in from left to right – Ed Stevens at first base, Eddie Stanky at second base, Pee Wee Reese at Short Stop, and Arky Vaughn and he played third base.

Left to Right – Ed Stevens, Warren Spahn, Pete Rose. This was me with two outstanding ball players. Warren is a hall of fame pitcher who I was noted for hitting well against (by him personally) years after we retired from playing. This was when I was a coach for San Diego.

Dixie Walker, an outstanding Brooklyn Dodger, and I were traded to Pittsburg at the same time.

Danny Murtaugh – I was known as "Big Ed"
but Danny liked to call me "Tex"

This is me and my teammates during Spring training in 1946 at our Havana Cuba facility.

The city of Galveston honored me by giving me a day, and a lot of gifts during one of our trips to Houston. This is while I was with Pittsburg and I made the short trip down to Galveston. A funny story about my attire – Back at that time the Texas Ranger Law Enforcement Officers dressed like this, and one day I decided to have a little fun. I walked into a place called the Turf Grill. I knew they had illegal gambling going on upstairs. As I walked in the front the cashier hit the button signaling the gambling room. All of the people came charging out of that room upstairs so they wouldn't get caught. One of the players was a friend of mine and he got all over me for playing the joke on them since I knew the cashier would think I was there to shut down the place.

Branch Rickey, who was the general manager during my days at Brooklyn.

Carl Furillo

Augie Galan

Leo Durocher

Kirby Higbee

Dixie Walker

Eddie Stanky

Pete Reiser

Pee Wee Reese

Ralph Branca

Cookie Lavagetto

Ed Stevens

Hugh Casey

Vic Lombardi

Hank Behreman

Ed Head.

Pitcher who learned to pitch with his right arm after suffering severe injury to his left arm, which was his natural throwing arm.

Phenomenal story because he threw a no hitter after the accident.

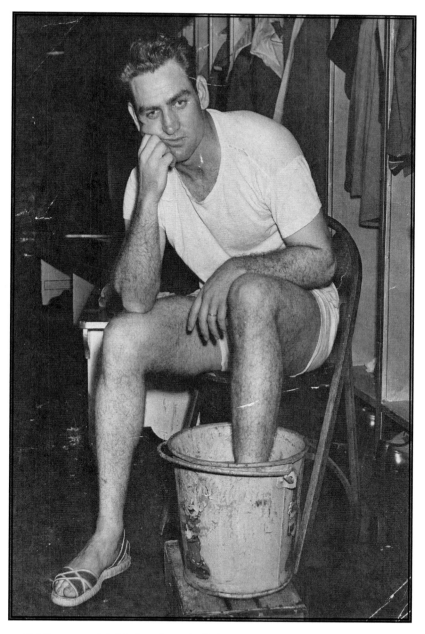

Ed Stevens with his "modern day" therapy treatment soaking a swollen ankle.

Ed Stevens and 3 of Bing Crosbys' sons. This is in Hollywood Ca. during Spring Training. Ed got a kick out of watching Bing and his boys all dress in the Pirate uniform to come out on the field.

This hand drawn picture was from an artist friend of mine during my first year in Pittsburgh.

Ed Stevens is number 4. This is an action shot of him that displays his noted ability to maintain great form even on some of the toughest throws. Ed had a .996 fielding percentage throughout his major league carrer.

STEVENS, EDWARD LEE

Born January 12, 1925, Galveston, Texas

Batted left. Threw left. Height 6.01. Weight, 190.

YEAR	CLUB	LEAGUE	POS	G
1941	Big Spring	West Texas-New Mexico	1B-OF	117
1942	Lamesa	West Texas-New Mexico	1B	64
	Johnstown	Pennsylvania State Assoc.	1B	46
1943		[Voluntarily Retired]		
1944	Montreal	International	1B	153
1945	Montreal	International	1B	110
	Brooklyn	National	1B	55
1946	Brooklyn	National	1B	103
1947	Brooklyn	National	1B	5
	Montreal	International	1B	133
1948	Pittsburgh	National	1B	128
1949	Pittsburgh	National	1B	67
1950	Pittsburgh	National	1B	17
	Indianapolis	American Association	1B	63
1951	Indianapolis	American Association	1B	152
1952	Toronto	International	1B	155
1953	Toronto	International	1B	151
1954	Toronto	International	1B	155
1955	Toronto	International	1B	66
1956	Toronto	International	1B	140
1957	Charleston	American Association	1B	105
	Rochester	International	1B	40
1958	Rochester	International	1B	123
1959	Dallas	American Association	1B	17
	Atlanta/Chattanooga	Southern	1B	60
1960	Atlanta (Coach)	Southern	[Did Not Play]	
1961	Mobile	Southern	1B	17
			Totals:	2242

Complied by Ray Nemec

AB	R	H	TB	2B	3B	HR	RBI	SB	PCT
462	81	125	200	24	6	13	74	10	.271
281	67	103	178	18	9	13	79	1	.367
176	28	48	73	10	3	3	21	2	.273
[Voluntarily Retired]									
543	77	147	240	37	4	16	102	5	.271
401	64	124	212	19	6	19	95	5	.309
201	29	55	87	14	3	4	29	0	.274
310	34	75	132	13	7	10	60	2	.242
13	0	2	3	1	0	0	0	0	.154
458	89	133	244	22	4	27	108	5	.290
429	47	109	170	19	6	10	69	4	.254
221	22	58	82	10	1	4	32	1	.262
46	2	9	11	2	0	0	3	0	.196
198	26	52	74	3	2	5	27	0	.263
575	85	150	221	21	7	12	91	0	.261
554	87	154	277	31	7	26	113	4	.278
520	82	146	233	20	5	19	92	6	.281
552	99	161	278	24	6	27	113	4	.292
236	35	65	95	7	1	7	42	3	.275
506	65	125	202	12	1	21	73	1	.247
370	46	84	156	20	2	16	45	1	.227
139	25	38	79	5	0	12	25	0	.273
415	54	109	180	23	3	14	47	2	.263
55	7	15	24	6	0	1	9	1	.273
204	21	47	72	11	1	4	23	1	.230
[Did Not Play]									
44	4	12	20	2	0	2	8	0	0.273
7909	1176	2146	3543	374	84	285	1380	58	0.271

Ed and Margie Stevens on their 66th wedding anniversary

ABOUT THE AUTHOR

Ed Stevens played first base for the Brooklyn Dodgers from 1945–1947. He was the first man to be replaced by a black player in the history of Major League Baseball. After that fateful '47 season, he was traded to the Pittsburgh Pirates, where he played from 1948–1950. After finishing out his career in Toronto, he served as a major league scout for twenty-nine years. Ed was later elected to the Brooklyn Dodger Hall of Fame, the International League Hall of Fame, the Texas Major League Scouts Hall of Fame, and the Baton Rouge Louisiana Kids Clinic Hall of Fame, where he served for forty years as a baseball instructor along with Mel Ott, Dizzy Dean, Ted Williams, Stan Musial, and Mickey Mantle.